INTEGRATED HAND
RESOURCES FOR MODERN EDUCATION

DAVID E. CORNEY

SENIOR LECTURER — NEWCASTLE COLLEGE OF ADVANCED EDUCATION, N.S.W., AUSTRALIA

A BELAIR PUBLICATION

FIRST PUBLISHED IN
GREAT BRITAIN 1985 BY
BELAIR PUBLICATIONS
LIMITED
PO BOX 12
TWICKENHAM TW1 2QL
ENGLAND

REPRINTED 1986 and 1987

© 1976 BY
DAVID E. CORNEY

PRINTED IN GREAT BRITAIN
BY BPCC GRAPHICS LTD.
SLACK LANE, DERBY
DE3 3FL

PUBLISHED IN AUSTRALIA BY
BELAIR PUBLICATIONS
PTY. LTD.
73 MADISON DRIVE,
ADAMSTOWN HEIGHTS,
N.S.W. 2289 AUSTRALIA

ISBN 0 947882 02 2

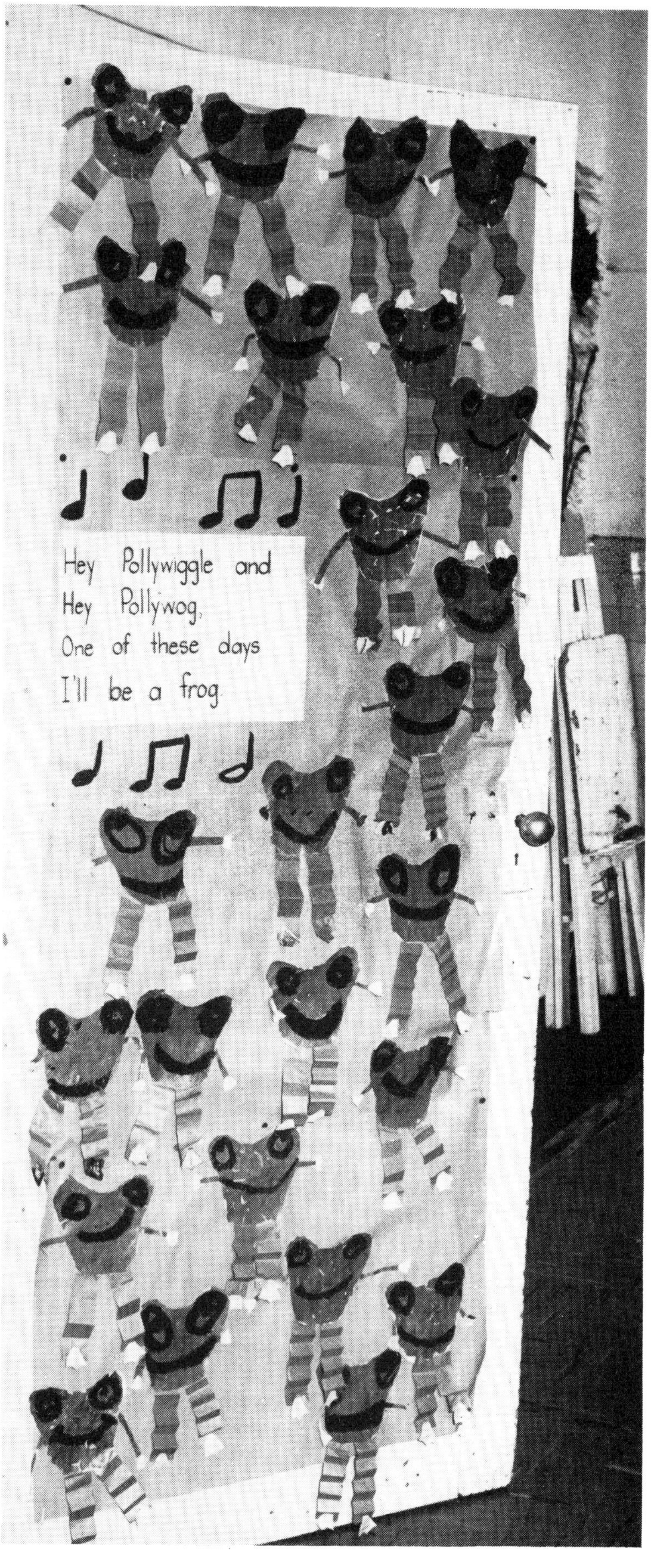

Hey Pollywiggle and
Hey Pollywog,
One of these days
I'll be a frog

INTEGRATED HANDWORK

DAVID E. CORNEY

WHERE TO FIND THINGS . . . . .

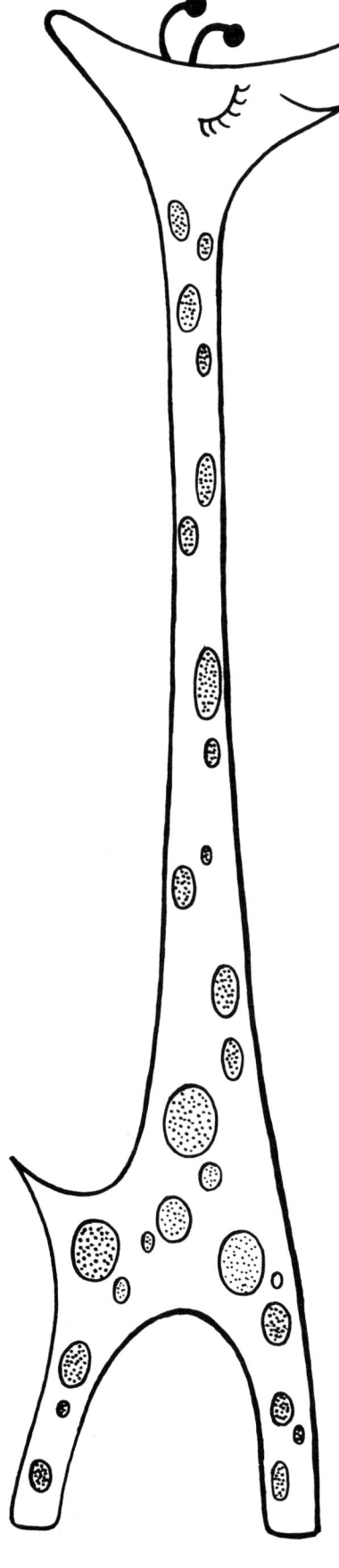

5	THANK YOU FOR HELPING
6	WHY INTEGRATE HANDWORK?
9	USING OUR SENSES TO LEARN
10	SIGHT
12	SOUND
15	SMELL
16	TOUCH
17	TASTE
19	LEARNING TO LOOK
20	DISCOVERING COLOUR
29	DISCOVERING SHAPE
36	DISCOVERING LINE
40	DISCOVERING TEXTURE
43	DEVELOPING PERCEPTUAL AWARENESS
45	ACHIEVING INTEGRATION THROUGH HANDWORK
47	WELCOME TO OUR CLASSROOM
48	ENVIRONMENTAL INFLUENCE
49	BLACK AND WHITE
51	SPEAKING OF COWS
56	HEALTH AND SAFETY
57	MAGIC
58	WITCHES
61	MAKE SOME MICE
64	POEMS AND RHYMES
68	PETS AND ANIMALS
73	EASTER ACTIVITIES
74	USING SCRAP MATERIALS
78	MAKE A CAKE SHOP
79	HANDWORK IS SOMETHING TO SING ABOUT

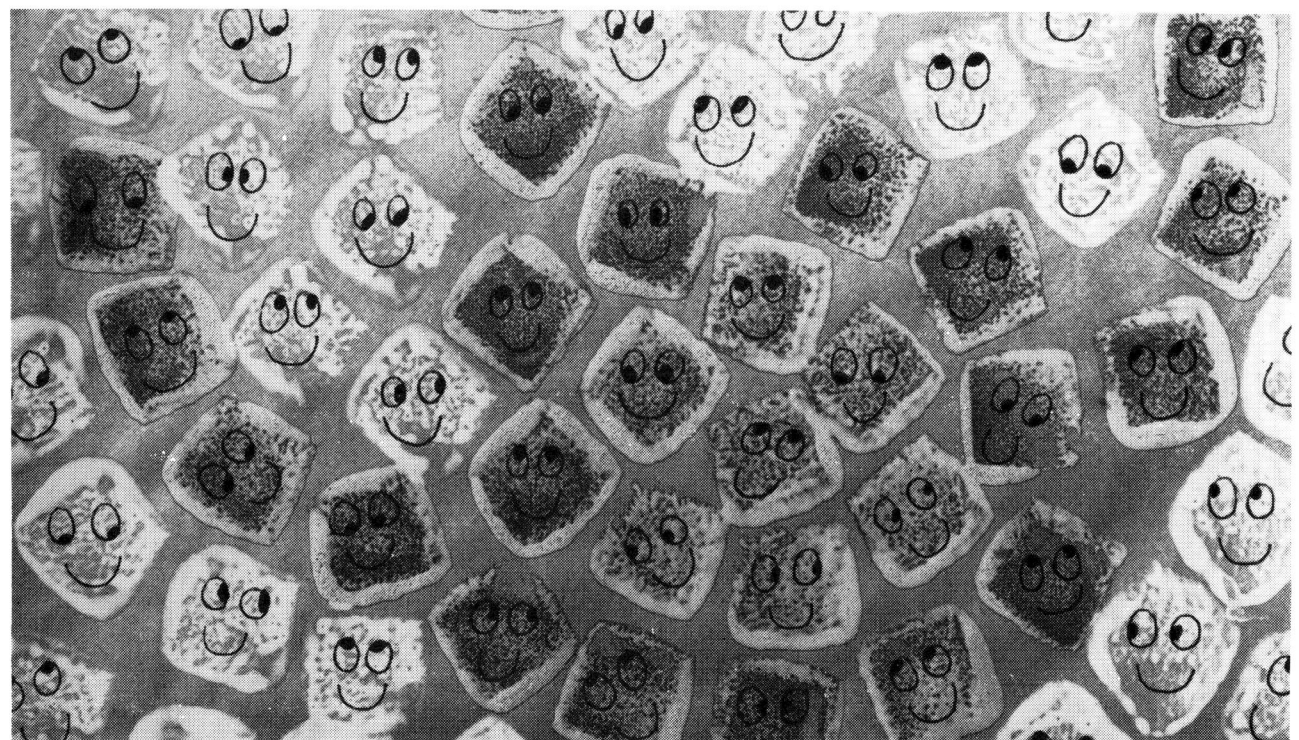

THANK YOU FOR HELPING . . . . .

Encouraged by the enthusiastic support received from teachers in all areas of Australia, INTEGRATED HANDWORK represents the ideas and efforts of many dedicated and talented teachers and teachers-in-training.

My first acknowledgement must be to the students at Newcastle College of Advanced Education with whom I have been privileged to work. Without their enthusiastic approach to the design and construction of the numerous experimental projects undertaken in recent years, many of the original activities, from which photographs and drawings have been prepared, would not have come into existence.

Secondly, I must acknowledge the friendly help and co-operation so generously extended by teachers in many parts of Australia. For permission to photograph children's work prepared under their guidance and for the opportunity of sharing ideas and opinions on the contribution of handwork to the everchanging role of education, I record my sincere appreciation.

Finally, in preparing the various areas of INTEGRATED HANDWORK, it has not been the intention of the author to infringe any existing copyright. Examples of material from a wide distribution of curriculum areas have been selected in an attempt to provide teachers with a range of approaches to the effective integration of handwork activities with subject content.

Should any of the material used be protected by copyright, the publisher would welcome information which would enable any omission of acknowledgement to be rectified in subsequent editions.

David E. Comey

WHY INTEGRATED HANDWORK . . . . .

How flexible is your teaching programme? Does a fixed and rigid timetable determine the activities and experiences the children will encounter during the course of the day or does the routine of your class provide sufficient flexibility to allow the children to derive the maximum benefit from the situations that may occur as involvement in one centre of interest leads to another?

What is to be achieved by putting off until its appointed time, something you could be doing right now, especially when it could add a real dimension of understanding to the Social Science project your class may be undertaking or perhaps serve to illustrate the information summarised from a film or T.V. programme.

In the total integration into subject content of manipulative skills and techniques, and of creative expression through the choice and use of materials and media, can be found the essence of Handwork. Only when Handwork is thought of in this way, can it realise its full potential as a contributor to the learning experience. Whether it takes the form of a painted mural, a construction from scrap materials, a mobile, a series of folded paper animals or involvement in a cooking activity, if it helps the children to gain greater understanding of the subject at hand then their involvement will be well justified.

In these times of educational change, terms such as Integrated Day and Open Classroom have become accepted forms of learning experience. Teachers have become increasingly aware that, if learning is to become fully effective, it must have significance and appeal to the child.

With this goal in mind, teachers are dismantling the barriers which have tended to place subjects in the regimented compartments of the past and are exploring new opportunities and experiences which allow subject content to achieve its greatest educational impact.

As an illustration of this approach, consider the example of a teacher who asked a group of young children to set up some work tables out in the sunshine, where the children could observe at first hand the magnificent shapes in the stance of trees growing at the edge of the playground and record their observations in the form of a collage with colours and textures torn from magazine advertisements.

Working without direction, the children positioned the tables in the shade of the foliage, then returned to their classroom where they and the teacher discussed some illustrations of different types of trees and how their appearance frequently indicates the season. The warm colours of the autumn foliage, the stark lines of deciduous trees in winter, the profusion of colour as blossom trees herald the arrival of spring and the shimmering green of willow trees in summer, were but a few of their observations.

Returning to their table to set about expressing their ideas the children exclaimed, "They've moved"!

"What's moved?" asked the teacher.

"The tables," replied the children. "They've moved out of the shade".

What would you have done if this had been your class? Continued with your planned collage activity or exploited the opportunity of the situation that had arisen in leading the children to an understanding of why the tables had "moved"? The teacher wisely chose the latter.

This was achieved by involving the children in activities which would lead to discovery. Stakes were placed in the ground and their shadows marked. Details of subsequent movement of the shadows were recorded.

The attention of the children was directed to their own shadows. They tried to jump on their shadow, shake hands with other shadows. One group made a shadow with six arms while another made a line of shadows which appeared as one shadow standing on the shoulders of another shadow.

Indeed, the day's activity had taken a different form from that which was originally planned but the children had gained much from their experience. The collage of the trees had given way to a new activity. Working in groups, the children painted their shadows on large sheets of paper and, when these were dry, cut around the shape they had recorded.

After lunch, other learning experiences emerged from their involvement in the morning's work. Some of the children wrote poems about their shadows.

"My shadow can run and jump and play,
But only on a sunny day", wrote six year old Anthony.

"My shadow is big and always black,
But doesn't have a front or back", contributed Louise.

Much had been achieved through the lesson on shadows and the achievement had been significant because the flexibility of the teacher's approach had enabled the most to be made out of an opportunity which had unexpectedly arisen. One discovery had led to another. Meaningful integration of several subject areas had been achieved.

In presenting INTEGRATED HANDWORK the author has endeavoured to present a wide selection of experiences to meet the needs and abilities of children in infant and primary grades.

Initially, involvement centres on the individual child's sensory response to his environment at school, at home and in the community beyond.

Activities designed to accentuate the awareness of the sense of sight, sound, touch, smell and taste have been suggested, as it has long been an established fact that all experience comes to the individual through the senses.

Some psychologists may wish to debate this statement, claiming that perception is sensation plus experience, yet few can deny that we perceive the world about us mostly through our eyes.

For this reason the "Discovering" activities are intended to help teachers lead children to an awareness of colour, shape, line and texture, the visual elements which identify the characteristics of the things we see around us in our everday encounters with the environment.

Undoubtedly, our eyes and the corresponding sense of vision provide the main avenue of learning experience and yet it does not necessarily follow that we understand what we see. For example, many children who are chronic television viewers with a characteristic glassy stare, see all, but receive very little. That is, they fail to understand what they see.

For there to be maximum learning, children must become actively involved in the learning experience and to this end the potential of Handwork is unlimited.

Perceptual awareness, developed through individual, group or class participation in the many types of activities suggested, is the ultimate goal of this book.

Activities are not graded or presented in any specific sequence, but are offered as a source of ideas and resources in order that the teacher may select those activities most appropriate to the ability of the children and the learning experience in which they are involved.

If integration and understanding are aided by the contents of the book then its contribution to education will be well worthwhile.

USING OUR SENSES TO LEARN . . . . .

LISTEN
Hear the sounds that surround us, people talking, music playing, birds singing, traffic rumbling.

LOOK
See the beauty of nature, flowers in bloom, a rainbow, animals grazing, a butterfly.

SMELL
Experience the aroma of freshly cut grass, a summer shower, food cooking, the ocean breeze.

TASTE
Savour the flavour of sweet, sour, salty or curried food.

TOUCH
Feel the surface of a mossy stone, a wet fish, a pineapple, a stringy bark tree trunk.

All of these experiences involve the use of our senses and help us to appreciate the world around us.

USING OUR SENSES.....

Children learn through their senses. They are the physical means by which all experience is transmitted to the child and yet few children possess the ability to look and SEE or listen and HEAR. There are so many things children take for granted and this applies particularly to their senses.

Training children to use and appreciate their senses is one of the most worthy goals a teacher can achieve. The identification of each sense and the role it plays in helping the child to discover more about his environment and the things in it, should be a prime objective.

To aid this development, the suggestions and activities that follow are intended to lead the children to experiences that will extend their sensory awareness and establish an ability to use their senses as a means of discovering things for themselves.

✱ Paint or construct a "life-size" model by tracing the outline of a boy or girl on a large sheet of paper. Identify ears, eyes, nose, mouth and hands with the appropriate related sense words.

This process of word association is an important aspect of all handwork activities and, wherever possible, some form of word or sentence structure should be displayed with the acitivity as an aid to the development of word recognition and reading skills. See previous page.

SIGHT.....

✱ Prepare a collection of visual experiences the children have enjoyed. This may take the form of pictures cut from old magazines or, preferably, paintings the children have prepared from past observations. Discuss scenes such as -

Fireworks exploding	**Autumn trees**
Boats under full sail	**Rainbow in the sky**
Sky at sunset	**Bonfires**
Stars twinkling at night	**Spider building a web**

Encourage children to identify those visual experiences which have particularly attracted their attention.

✲ Read the fun poem "Boggly Blogg". Suggest that the children try to create "Boggly Blogg" by painting or constructing from scrap materials.

THE BOGGLY BLOGG

The Boggly-blogg has no eyes,
Cannot see, though hard he tries,
Sunsets, stars or butterflies.

The Boggly-blogg has no ears,
So not a single sound he hears -
No singing, laughter, sobs or cheers.

The Boggly-blogg has no nose,
And therefore, as you may suppose,
Can't tell an onion from a rose.

Without a tongue he's badly placed,
To recognise the simplest taste,
For him a feast is just a waste.

And naturally he sorrows much,
To learn, without a sense of touch,
Mud, sand and fur the same to clutch.

Just think about poor Boggly's case,
For him the world's a nothing place.
I'm glad I'm from the human race.

✲ On a more serious note, discuss the problems of people who are deprived of the use of their senses, particularly blind or deaf people.

Indicate some of the ways these people use their other senses, which often become so highly developed that they compensate for the missing sense.

Blind people learn to read with their finger tips — sense of touch.
Deaf people learn to lip read — sense of sight.
Examine other methods of communication used by blind and deaf people.

SOUND . . . . .

* Discuss different sounds the children have especially noticed. Encourage them to comment on their response at the time of hearing these sounds.

    Roosters crowing   Wind in the trees
    Rain on the roof   The siren on an ambulance
    Thunder   A dripping tap at night
    Birds singing at sunrise   Screeching brakes of a car

* Draw or model something that makes a distinctive sound.

* Have groups of children prepare a tape of sounds to be identified by other children. Encourage the use of everyday experiences such as:-

Telephone ringing	Musical instruments
Clock ticking	Door closing
Dog barking	Whistle
Traffic noises	Cutting with scissors
Cutlery clinking	Jiggling money
Winding a clock	Cow mooing
Food mixer	Motor lawnmower
Approaching footsteps	Hammering a nail
Water running	Baby crying
Kettle whistling	Door bell

* Make some simple musical instruments

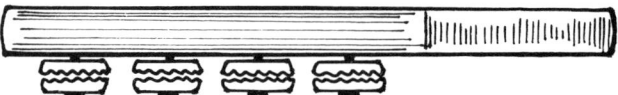

Nail bottle tops to a strip of wood to make a jingle stick.

Glue sandpaper to offcuts of wood to make a set of sandblocks.

* Make a paper cup or tin-can telephone. Attach about 6 metres of string to each cup through a small hole pierced in the bottom. Keep string under tension as children experiment with the various ways of transmitting sounds.

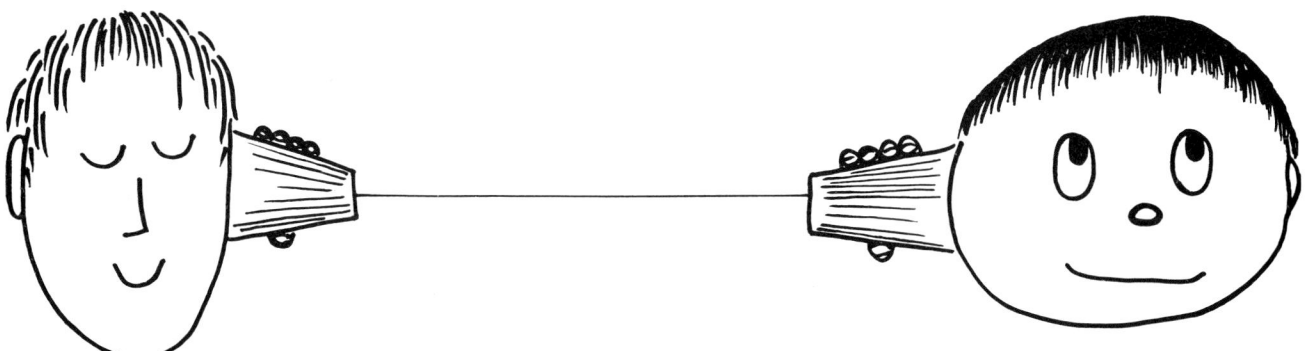

* Fill several identical glass tumblers or milk bottles with different amounts of water. Tap the glass lightly with a pencil and notice the sound. See if you can play a tune on the glasses.

* Make a list of words that tell us about noises -

splash	echo	bang	clang	rustle	yell
sizzle	scream	boom	roar	clatter	shout
crash	hiss	thud	whisper	groan	rumble
flap	whistle	tinkle	cheep	moan	patter
thump	clap	quack	moo	drip	yap
rattle	hubbub	slam	crack	honk	toot
tick-tock					

* Draw your own picture to illustrate one of the noise words from the list compiled by the class.

* Choose the word you associate with the illustrations.

* Use animated figures to represent the members of the City Band.
  Discuss the sounds made by the various instruments of the band.

* Compose a poem about noise.

* Read poems about sounds.

The quack of a duck, the thud of a hoof,
The patter of rain on a galvanised roof,
The hubbub of traffic, the roar of a train,
The scream of a siren, piercing the brain.
From the stillness of silence that sound destroys,
Rises a gamut of soul-stirring joys.

TICK TOCK
Tick Tock
Calls the clock,
Telling the time
All by itself.
Round and round
The two hands go,
The big one quickly,
The little one slow.

NOISES
The loudest noise I ever heard -
It was a train that puffed and grunted,
As along the tracks it shunted.
Roaring loudly on its way,
It must have had a lot to say.

The softest noise I ever heard -
It was a teeny, weeny mouse,
As he scampered to his house.
He sat so still behind the wall,
I hardly heard his noise at all.

SMELL.....

✼ Discuss distinctive smells the children have noticed.

New shoes	Freshly cut grass
Fresh bread baking	The ocean spray
Inside a new car	Old books
Closed up rooms	Onions frying
The air after a summer storm	Wet paint
Perfume	A dairy farm
Dad's after-shave lotion	Freshly ground coffee
Hot tar	Cigar smoke
Wet wool	Ripe apples

✼ Make some large paper flowers and attach an area of coloured felt, cotton wool, or fabric to the centre of each unit. Sprinkle a few drops of different identifiable aromas on each of the flowers to arouse the children's sense of smell.
Suitable substances include -

Peppermint essence	Camphor
Eucalyptus oil	Vapour rub
Perfume	After-shave lotion

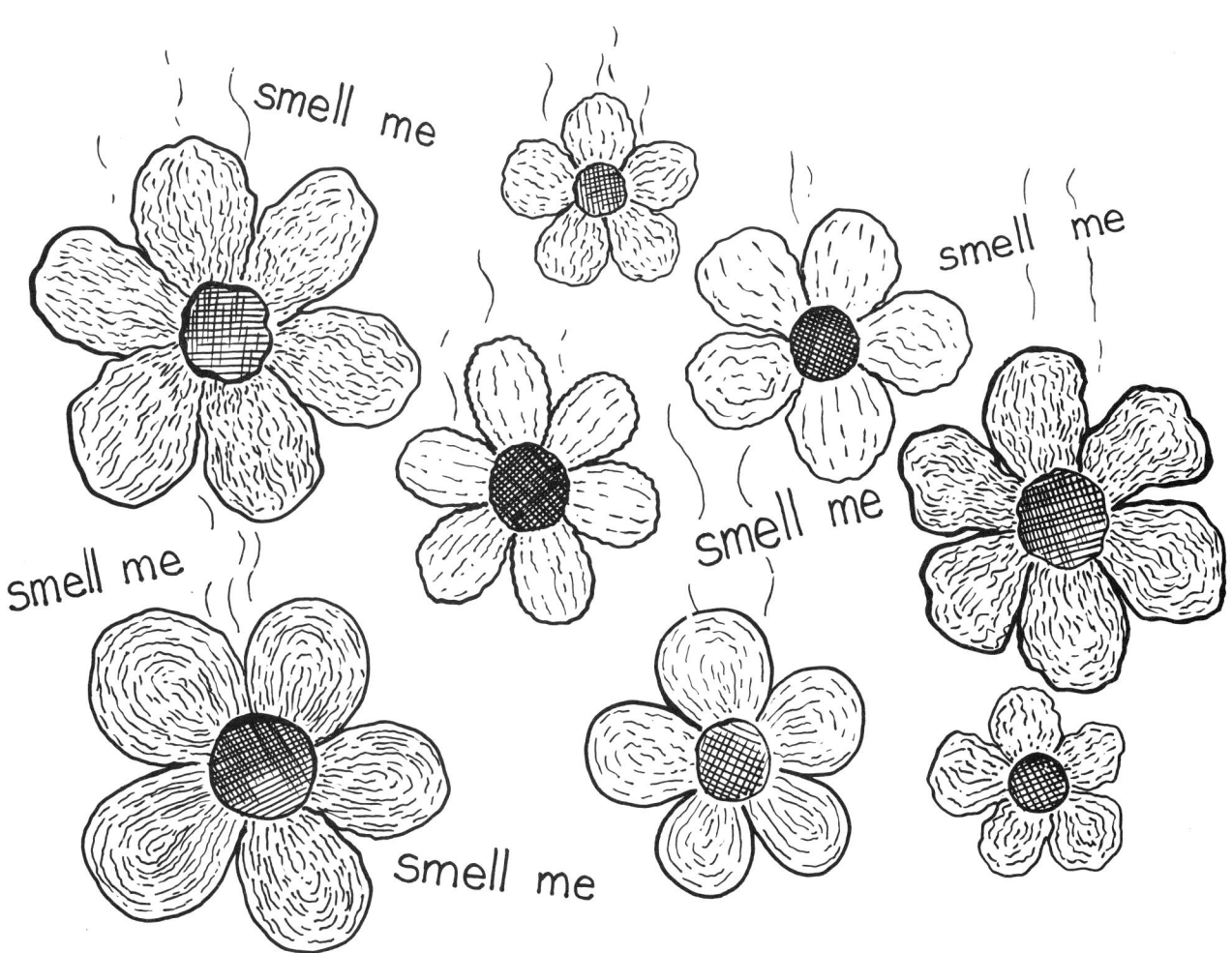

TOUCH.....

* Discuss things the children have experienced as having an unusual sensation to touch -

A wet fish	**A real beard**
Skin of a peach	**Sandpaper**
Animal fur	**Food grater**
Velvet	**Modelling clay**
Skin of a baby	**Dough**

* Are there any surfaces they do not like to touch?   **Greasy   Hot   Slimy**

* Having discussed the sensation of touch, encourage children to express their ideas in the form of creative writing.

SOFT
Soft as a kitten,
Soft as a rainbow's colour,
Soft as a down feather,   This example is the work of a 7 year old girl.
Soft as melted butter,
Soft as clean hair,
A loving smile and Mum's perfume,
Soft keeps you warm and cosy too,
It feels lovely.
                                    Narelle

* Make a texture board. Using a suitable backing and an appropriate adhesive such as P.V.A., bond a variety of textured materials in squares on the board. Prepare smaller areas of the same texture on separate pieces of thick cardboard.
  Relying on their sense of touch, have the children match the textures.

* Prepare a mural which provides scope for the application of different textured materials. In the example below notice the variety of textures in the foliage of the trees.

TASTE.....

* Prepare lists of taste sensations. Set out one list showing taste experiences the children have enjoyed and another showing those they have disliked.
  Another approach is to list substances that have different types of taste, e.g.

SWEET	Sugar Honey Mint	SOUR	Lemon Vinegar Grapefruit	HOT	Curry Pepper Mustard

* Make a giant class cooking book in preparation for the children's involvement in a cooking activity. Discuss the recipe, ingredients to be purchased, utensils required and method of serving the finished product, so that all appropriate information can be recorded in the book prior to the actual activity.
  The size of the class and facilities available will influence the type of activity to be selected, however the following suggestions may be appropriate -

Vegetable salad (prepared by children) - e.g. carrots, celery, cauliflower, cucumber, green pepper, dressing.
Cress (grown by children) for egg and cress sandwiches.
Mung beans (grown by class).

JAM TARTS
200g. 8oz. S.R. flour
pinch of salt
50g. 2oz. lard
50g. 2oz. margarine
cold water to mix
* Mix flour and salt, rub in lard and margarine.
* Mix in cold water to form a stiff paste.
* Turn onto board and roll out.
* Cut into rounds and place in patty tins.
* Put a little jam in each.
* Bake for 15 minutes Gas Mark 6, 400°F. 200°C.

CHEESE STRAWS
100g. 4oz. S.R. flour
pinch of salt
pinch of mustard
50g. 2oz. margarine
75g. 3oz. hard cheese, grated
1 egg, beaten
* Sieve the flour, salt and mustard. Rub in margarine.
* Mix in cheese and add sufficient egg to make a stiff dough.
* Roll out very thinly and cut in strips. Place on a greased tray.
* Bake at Gas Mark 4, 350°F. 18°C. for 10-15 minutes.

CHOCOLATE CRACKLES
100g. 4oz. margarine
2 tbs. syrup
2 tbs. cocoa
50g. 2oz. coconut
150g. 6oz. puffed rice cereal
* Melt the margarine, syrup and cocoa in a pan.
* Add the coconut and puffed rice. Mix well.
* Spoon the mixture into paper cases.

POTATO AND CARROT SOUP
450g. 1lb. potatoes
450g. 1lb. carrots
1 stock cube
300ml. ½ pt. hot water
600ml. 1pt. milk
salt and pepper
* Peel and chop the potato and carrot, put in a large pan.
* Add the stock cube, water, milk, salt and pepper.
* Simmer for 20 minutes until cooked.

CLASS COOK BOOK

On inside pages show ......

shopping list . . .

* flour
* margarine
* sugar

things we'll need

* clean hands
* scales
* mixing bowl
* knife
* pastry board or work surface
* round or square baking tin

RECIPE FOR SHORTBREAD

* 175g. 6oz. plain flour
  100g. 4oz. hard margarine
  50g. 2oz. sugar

* Place all ingredients in a large mixing bowl.
  Chop margarine and rub in with fingertips.

* Knead to form a ball.

* Pat out onto greased tin.

* Bake at Gas Mark 4, 350°F. 180°C. for 20-25 minutes.

LEARNING TO LOOK.....

In contemporary society, ever-increasing amounts of information and ideas are being presented in visual form.

Apart from the abundance of signs, symbols, advertisements, books, magazines and packages that children observe, they are also viewing substantial amounts of film and television.

The ultimate influence of this exposure tends to be that children are looking more and seeing less. That is, their eyes perform the physical actions of recording an image yet their brain makes little attempt to register the detail of what has been observed.

There are occasions, however, when children do pay special attention to a visual experience which holds some significant appeal. "Look at that" or "Isn't that nice" might be the response used to identify such an occasion.

This is where the alert teacher can lead children to an understanding of what they see. When children exhibit a response to a visual stimulus, they are indicating that there are certain qualities of their visual experience that appeal to their senses.

It may be a relationship of colour, shape, line, texture or a combination of these. Whatever it is, through thoughtful discussion and the presentation of appropriate experiences, the skilful teacher can help children isolate the various elements they see and progressively establish an understanding of their contribution to the surrounding environment.

In the pages that follow, the elements of colour, shape, line and texture have been isolated and activities suggested which will provide opportunities for the children to use their senses in appreciating these elements: at the same time they will be acquiring skills and techniques in giving visual form to information gathered from all areas of learning experience.

DISCOVERING COLOUR.....

COLOUR IN NATURE

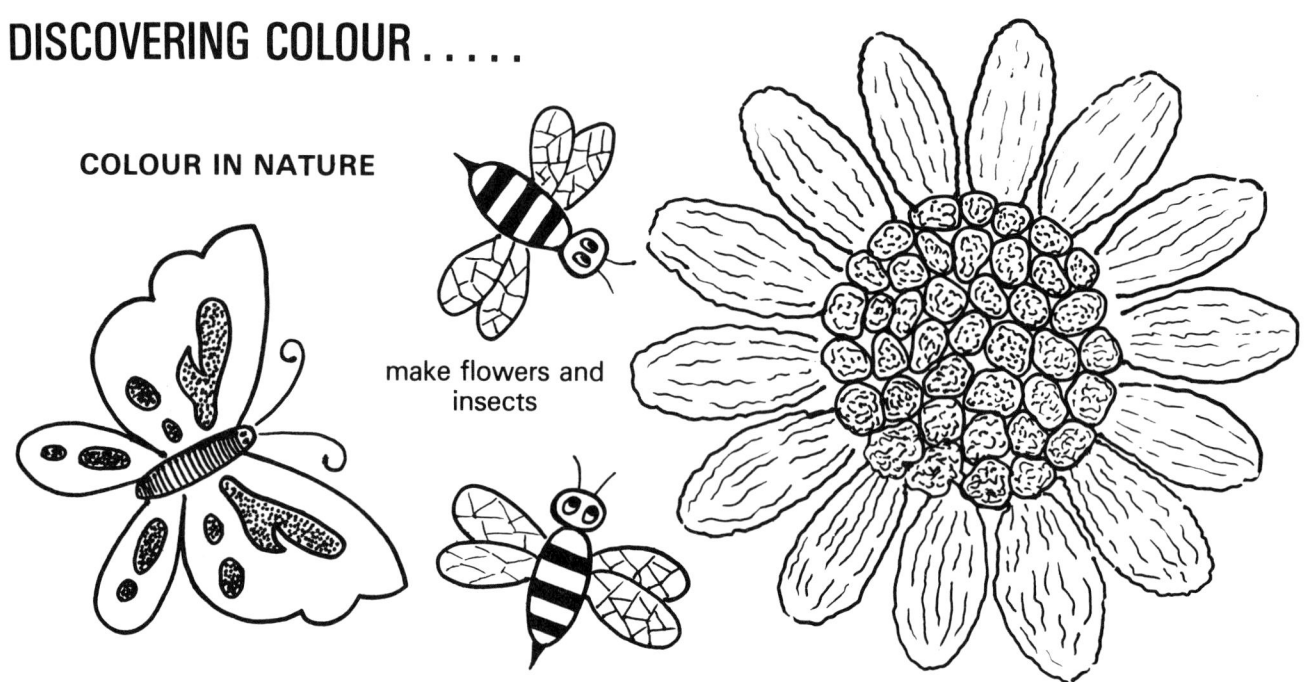

make flowers and insects

* Bright colours of flowers attract insects which play an important role in transferring pollen from one flower to another.

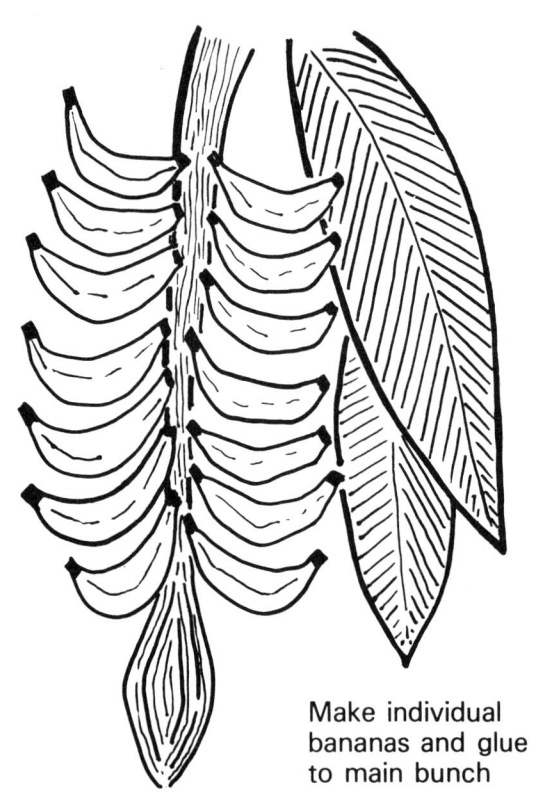

Make individual bananas and glue to main bunch

* Colours tell us when fruit is ripe and ready to eat.

I am little Miss Apple,
My home is in a tree,
Way up in the branches
Where nobody can see
My cheeks are so rosy
My skin is so white,
I know I am juicy
So please~take a bite!

✱ Colours tell us a good deal about the seasons we experience.

> **AUTUMN**
> Tumble Down, tumble down,
> Leaves of yellow, gold and brown,
> Tumble, tumble all around,
> Make a carpet on the ground.

Blend colours of crepe paper to make trees representing the seasons.

AUTUMN	SPRING	SUMMER
Yellow	Pink	Dark Green
Gold	White	Light Green
Brown	Red	Lemon
Orange		

Twist strips of crepe paper and hang half lengths to represent the foliage. Use full lengths of light and dark brown to suggest the trunk.

An alternate method is to use all full lengths of various tones. This is most effective for willow trees, waterfalls or underwater effects.

✱ Colours can also act as a warning. Here are some examples. Can you think of others?

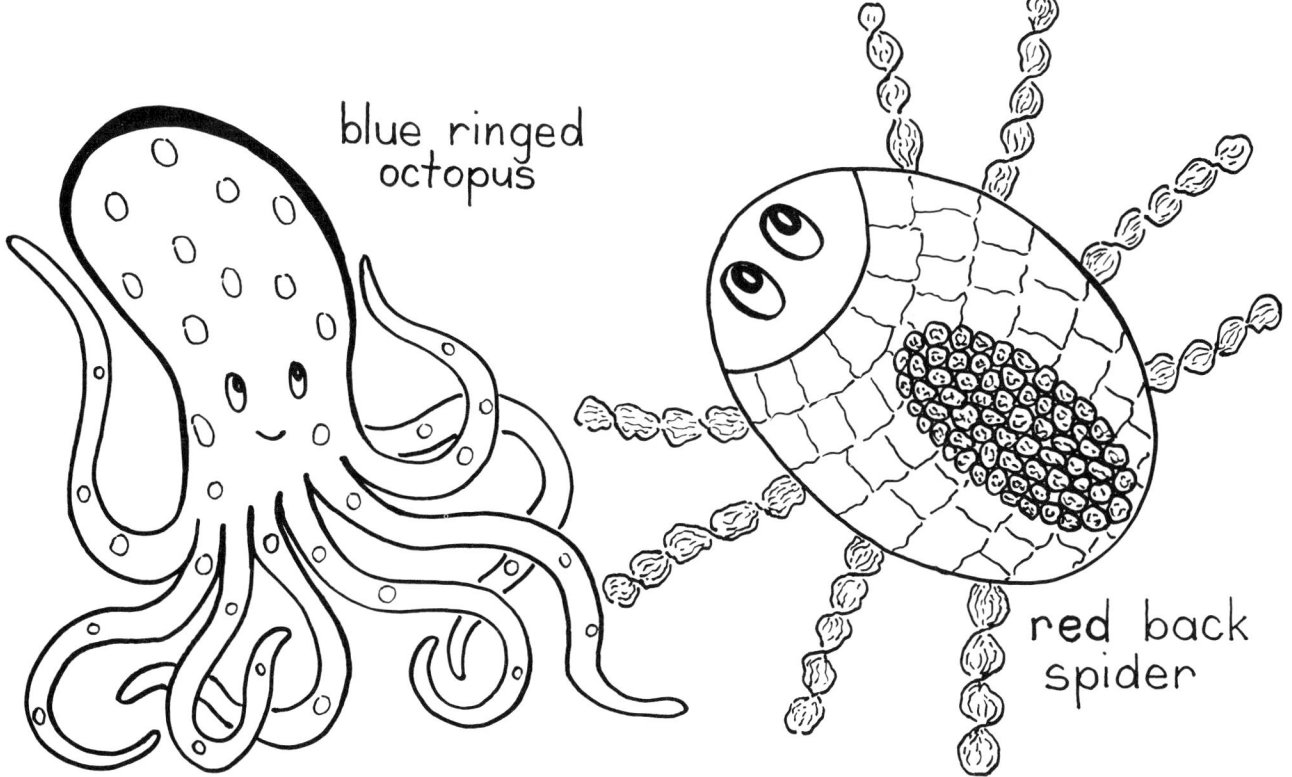

blue ringed octopus

red back spider

* Many creatures are coloured in such a way as to help them blend in with the colours of their surrounding environment. This is called camouflage. The lion uses his camouflage to help him creep up on animals he is trying to catch. Other creatures use their camouflage to hide themselves from enemies. This is their only form of protection.

Encourage children to conduct independent research as a means of establishing a pool of information and ideas which can be given form through handwork activities.

* Most colours appear either warm or cool when we look at them. Red, yellow and orange remind us of hot things, like fire or sunsets, so we call them warm colours.

Cool colours are the blues and greens that remind us of cool running water, shady trees or grassy fields.

In our environment, mostly cool colours appear. The blue sky, green trees and plants. These are restful colours.
In the waterfall shown opposite children have used a mixture of cool colours to represent the cascading water.

Apart from studying the colours of the water, they have been learning about the energy that exists in falling water and how this energy is used to generate electricity.

COLOURS PEOPLE USE

✻ Just as colours serve different functions in nature, people, too, use colours for similar purposes. Bright colours like red and yellow are used to attract attention. They are easy to see and stand out from most other colours.

Make a list of all the different ways people use colours to attract attention.

Fire engines	Advertisements	Post Boxes
Ambulances	Packets in shops	Bulldozers
Police cars	Yellow raincoats	Ski clothes
Taxis	Litter bins	Beach umbrellas
Buses	Circus vans	Tee Shirts
Road signs	Posters	Flags
Road markings	Bus stops	Neon signs
Lifejackets	Food wrappers	Life rafts

✻ As well as attracting attention, special colours like red are used to warn of danger.

* Colour is often used as a means of identification.

Taxis stand out from other cars.
People in many shops wear coloured uniforms so the customer will know who to ask for help.
Police, Firemen, Nurses, Bus Drivers and most people who serve a special function in the community wear a distinctive uniform.
Sporting teams choose different colours so each player can identify his team-mates.

* Make a list of other examples of where colour is used for identification.

* Divide the class into two groups. Prepare figures to represent teams wearing different identifying colours.

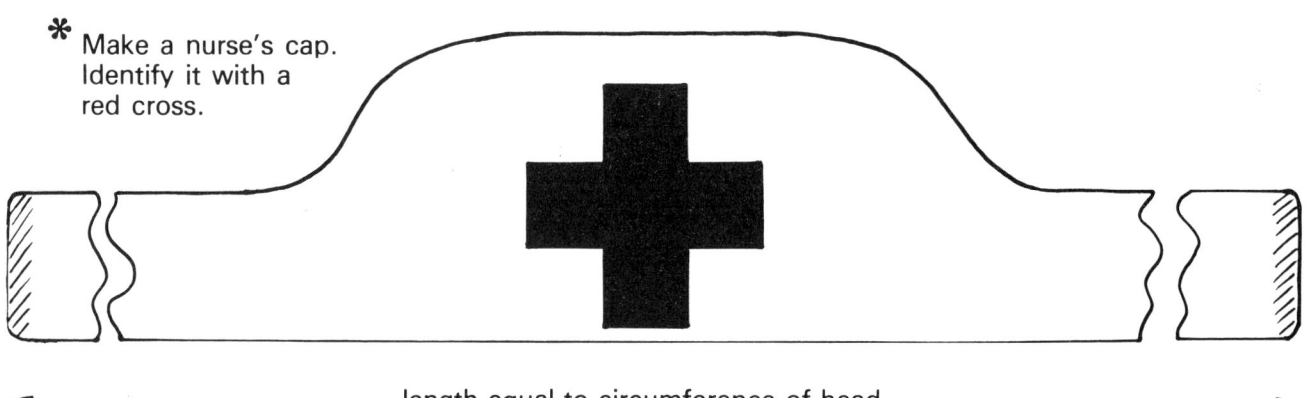

* Make a nurse's cap. Identify it with a red cross.

length equal to circumference of head

* Paint a street scene. Use bright colours to identify cars, people, signs, etc. (see next page).

* As well as examining the use of colours in nature and in man's service, there are many other activities which help children to establish an awareness of colour. These include -

Obtain several paint colour cards from a local hardware store. Have the children choose colours they would use for specific purposes, e.g., paint their bedroom, paint outside their home, paint a dog kennel.

Examine the range of colours available for a current model car. Have the children imagine that their family is about to buy a new car and they have to choose the colour. Allow each child to paint the shape of a car and colour it to indicate his choice. Make a bar graph, on a class basis, of the results. Discuss reasons for their choice.

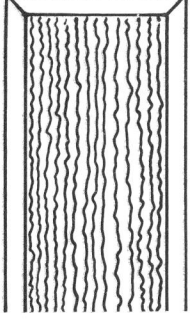

* Make a door curtain for your classroom of a selected colour range. Use two or three tones of the one colour. Cut strips from rolls of crepe paper and twist. Attach twisted strips to top of architrave with masking tape.

* Establish a colour interest centre in one corner of the room. Use pictures cut from magazines. Paintings in one colour. Colour collage in scrap materials. Trees or flowers made from the selected colour.

As a variation of above, several colour centres can be established, or warm - cool areas can be created.

✱ Have a "colour party" - Divide children into groups of designated colours. Red. Green, Orange. Prepare party hats, table novelties, balloons and streamers of the appropriate colour.
Serve coloured drink, food and sweets.
As a safety precaution avoid the use of blue, since this colour is used to identify kerosene. Discuss the use of colour to identify dangerous liquids.

✱ Conduct experiments in mixing paint. With older children, introduce shades and tints by the addition of black and white. Have children match colours to correspond with those printed on a paint colour-card.

✱ Prepare a colour-word chart. Have children identify colours that they associate with specific words.
e.g. Angry - Red   Busy   Cold
      Happy - Yellow   Important   Lazy
      Sad - Dk. Blue   Hot   Annoying
      Lonely - Brown   Impatient   Fast

✱ Fold a sheet of paper in half and place a few drops of different coloured paint on the fold, or to one side of the fold. Close the paper and apply a light pressure to the outside. This will cause the paint to merge and form new shapes and colours inside. Open the paper to its original area and encourage the children to discuss the shapes they have formed.

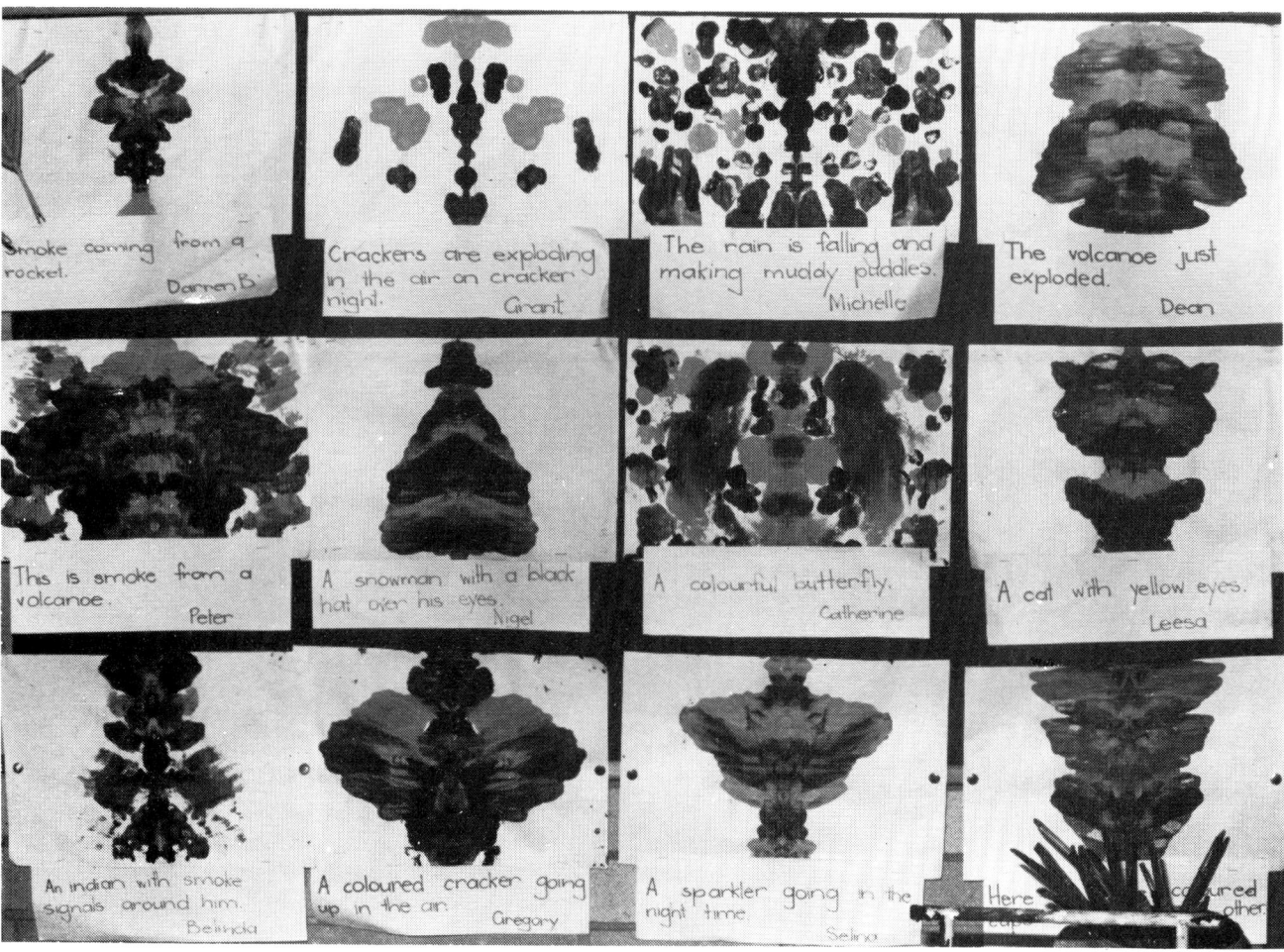

* Many interesting effects can be achieved by working with transparent coloured materials such as tissue or cellophane paper.

In the examples below, the fish have been made by winding a length of cotton around the point at which the cane crosses, then, to eliminate the need for knotting the cotton, glue it to the cane. This shape is then glued onto the tissue or cellophane and allowed to dry, after which the surplus is trimmed away.

In other activities, the designs are cut from black paper and areas of coloured translucent or transparent material glued underneath.

✱ Frequently poems about colour help children to appreciate the influence of the colour in our environment.

A worthwhile reference for an excellent collection of poems about colour is HAILSTONES AND HALIBUT BONES, by Mary O'Neill. The one set out below is similar to those in the book.

WHAT IS RED?

Red is a bushfire
Blazing and bright,
Red is like running
With all of your might.
Red is the sunburnt
End of your nose,
Often red
Is a lovely rose.
Red oozes out
When you scratch your hand.
Red is the sound
Of a passing brass band.
Red is the feeling
You get inside,
When you're embarrassed
And want to hide.
Red is a traffic-light,
Red is a shout,
Red is a warning
That says: "Watch out!"
Red is a spinning
Cricket ball.
Red is the brightest
Colour of all.
Red is a show-off,
No doubt about it -
But life would be drab
Living without it.

✱ When selecting coloured materials for painting or handwork activities, choose a variety of tones which suggest the movement of light. In the scene of the "Three Little Pigs" below, notice the effective use of the tonal variation in the formation of the trees.

✱ Encourage children to write or appreciate stories and poems about colour.

COLOURS

I see many colours
As I move around,
Motor cars and buses,
Flowers on the ground.
Sky and trees and buildings,
Clothes and bags and hats,
Different coloured animals,
Birds and fish and cats.
Sailing ships on water,
Fire engines too,
Orange, red and purple,
Yellow, green and blue.
Colour in the city,
Colour where I play,
Colour all around me
Somewhere everyday.

DISCOVERING SHAPE . . . . .

Wherever something that has a strong light behind is viewed, it no longer appears as a detailed object but as a silhouette or shape.
There is a great deal to be learnt about the use of shape in design because, whenever children draw or paint or construct, they are using shapes of one form or another.
The activities that follow are intended to make children more aware of shape, whether it be abstract or concrete, and of its role in visual communication.

*   A good starting point is to look at the shapes we can make with our hands and feet. If a sand pit is available, study the shapes made by feet walking across the sand. Examine some of the information to be gathered from the footprints, such as direction, size and weight. Discuss shapes made by shoes, birds, animals.
Place a quantity of water-base paint on a piece of foam or felt in the bottom of a shallow tray. Allow children to "ink" their feet and walk across a paper surface. (see page 33).

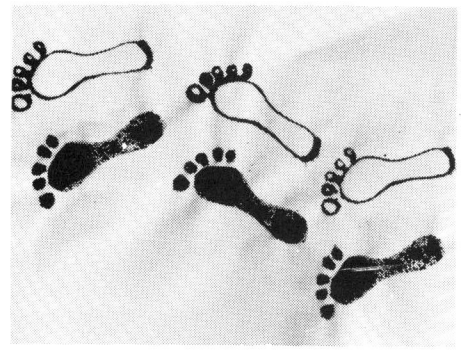 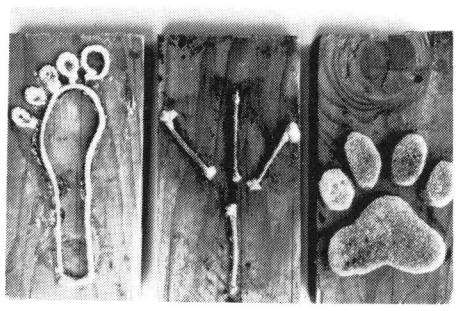 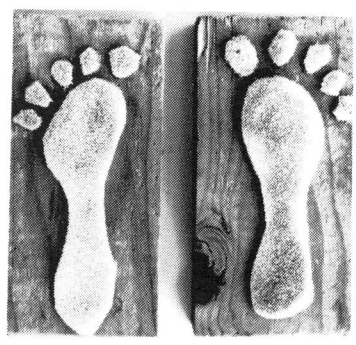

* Print shapes of animal or human "footprints" by cutting shapes from thin foam plastic and gluing to suitably sized wooden support blocks. Brush paint onto the surface of the foam and print. As an alternative method, outline shapes with string as shown above.

* Collect photographs and illustrations of city buildings. Examine the variety of shapes that exist.

* Cut shapes from paper and glue to painted cardboard boxes to form a model city or make a mural of city buildings from paper shapes.

* Look for patterns of shape made by quantities of similar types of objects. This stack of pipes is an example.

* Design a "family of shapes". These can be drawn and cut from coloured paper or prepared as a potato print and printed in various colours. (see page 33).

* Make a mobile of shapes. Cut shapes from heavy, dark coloured paper. Colour open areas with cellophane or tissue.

* Design a "Rooster" from simple shapes.

In most handwork activities the opportunity exists for combining the various elements. Once children understand the concept of one element, such as colour, the understanding can be applied to another element, such as shape. On this page and the next, examples of activities which combine colour and shape are represented.

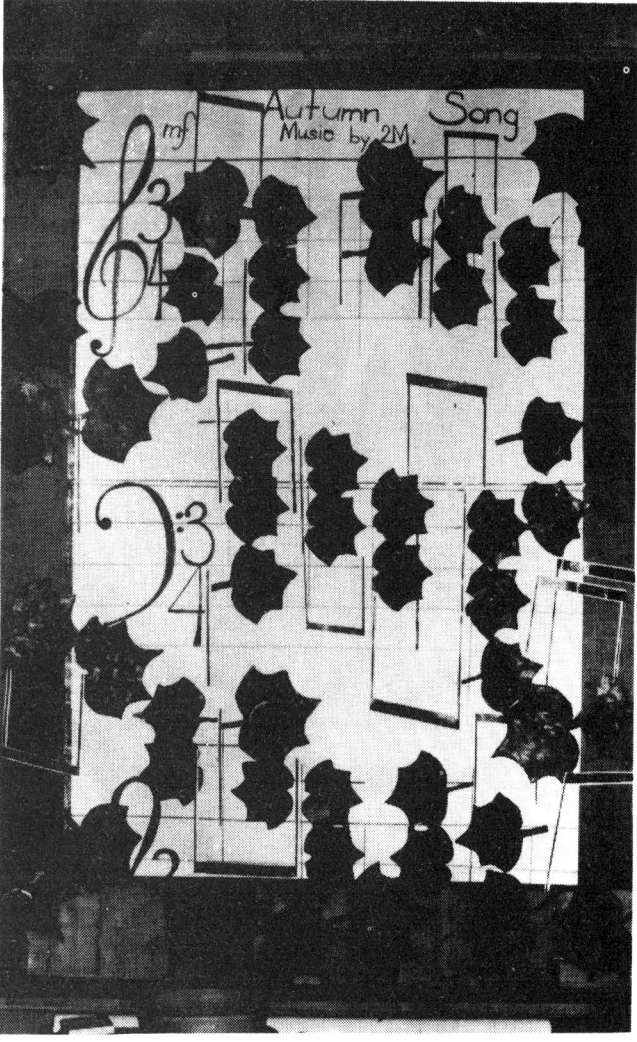

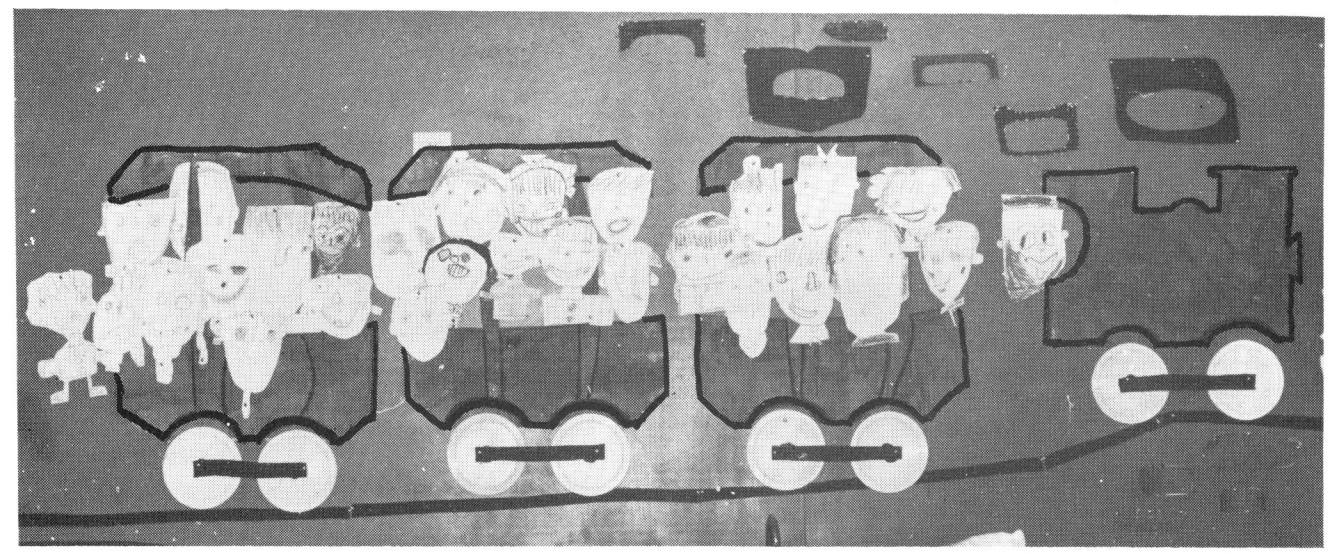

* Design a soft-edge shape

* Design a hard-edge shape.

* Most things we see in our environment can be represented as a shape. This technique is used by designers who create the signs and symbols that can be understood by people who speak many different languages. Can you understand the meaning of the shapes below?

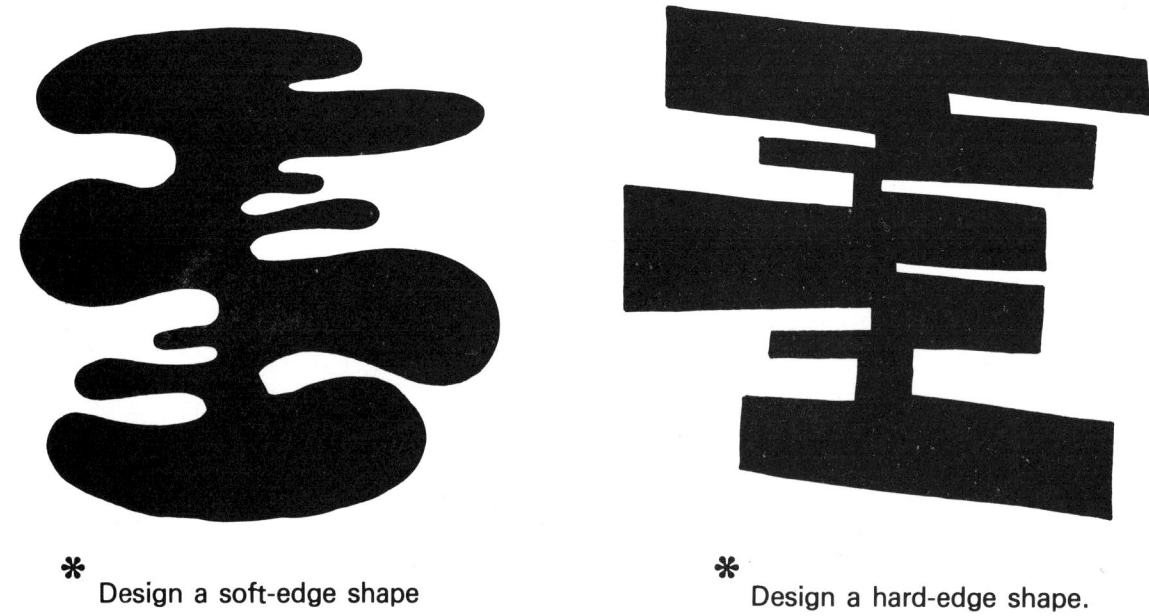

✱ Frequently the development of an awareness of an element can be related to specific themes or stories the children may be experiencing. This is the case in the two activities shown below. In the first, the shape of the balloons has emerged from a study of the theme of "Air" and in the second, a delightful variety of shapes has been used to illustrate the "Jack-in-the-Box" story.

DISCOVERING LINE . . . . .

One of the most expressive of all the visual elements is line. Straight or curved, thick or thin, its infinite variety of forms enables it to be used in a multitude of ways. Whether we see it in the delicate threads of a spider's web or the steel framework of a huge ferris wheel, it can lead our eyes on a memorable journey of visual experience.

* Collect illustrations of examples of line in natural and man-made forms.

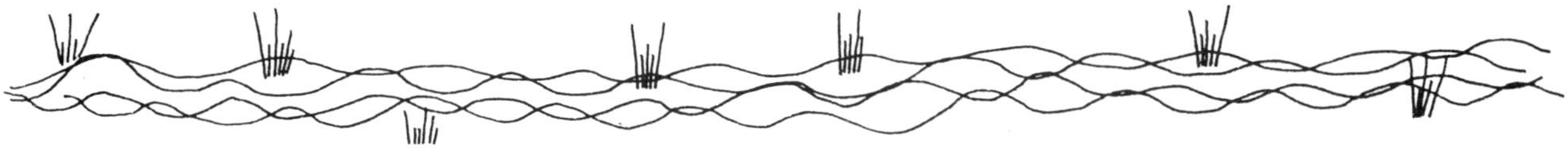

A stream flowed by at a steady pace

* Examine some of the ways we use line to express our ideas and communicate with others. Line is used to represent shapes when we draw or to form the letters of words when we write. Pre-writing exercises are examples of gaining control in the use of line as the forerunner to printing and writing.

* Experiment with various techniques which produce different types of line.

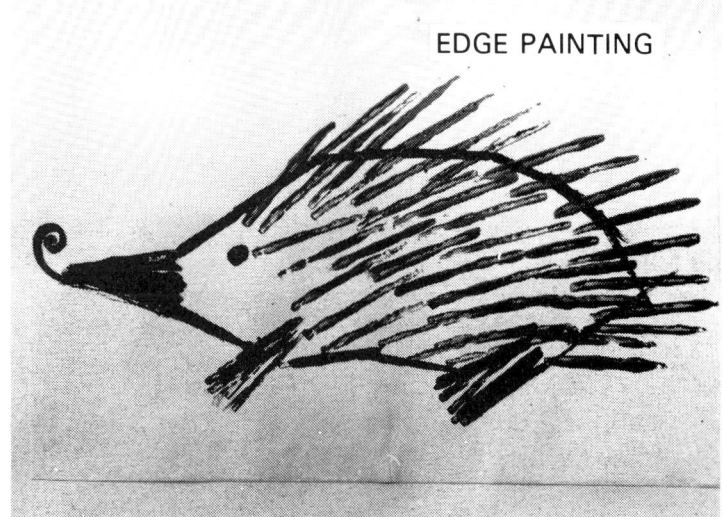

Place a few drops of thin paint on the surface of the paper and move them in different directions by blowing a jet of air through a drinking straw.

Using the lid of an ice-cream can as a container, pour a little paint onto a piece of foam plastic or fabric. Press the edge of a piece of stiff cardboard onto the paint then print the edge on paper. Repeat this process to produce different linear designs or pictures.

* Many surfaces such as wool, fur, hair or feathers can be suggested by the free flowing, repetitive use of line. Here are some examples.

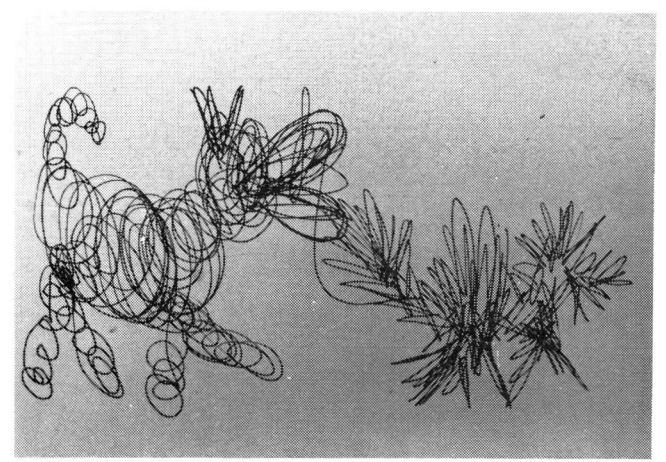

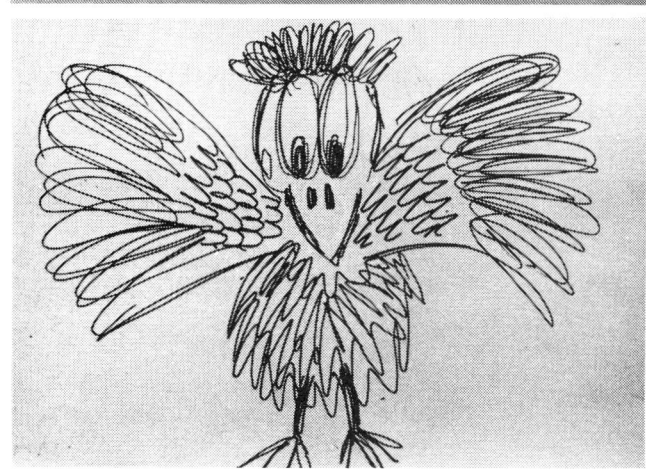

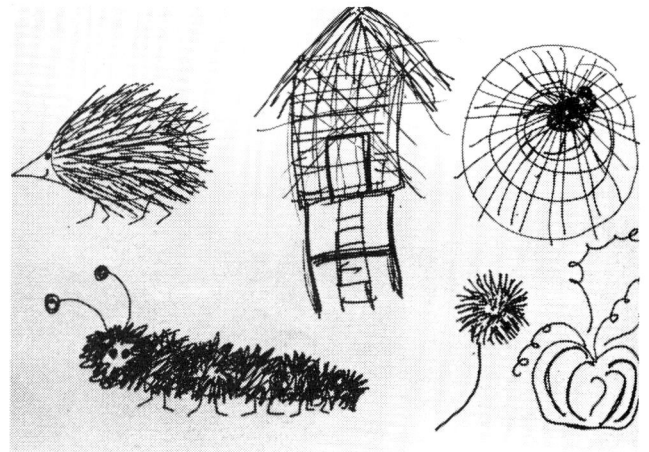

* Use paint or a felt pen to represent the linear form of a dried arrangement. Add twisted crepe paper blossoms.

* An alternate method is to model a miniature tree using the lid of a spray can as the base. This is filled with plasticine or plaster of paris which in turn supports the dried branches of the blossom tree.

* Take a line for a walk — Start with a dot; as the dot moves, it forms a line. Create as many interesting visual effects as possible.

DISCOVERING TEXTURE.....

Many teachers tend to think that texture is a term which relates exclusively to the sense of touch. A surface may feel smooth or rough, but this is only the tactile form of texture. There is also a visual form of texture, in which surfaces appear smooth or rough to the sense of sight. Surfaces which are rough to touch are generally rough in appearance, yet many soft materials such as cotton wool, plastic foam and fabric can be used to suggest a rough visual texture.

Texture can also be implied by the use of colour, shape and line so it is extremely important that teachers and children develop a sensitivity to the use of texture. Many large-scale activities such as murals and posters can lose their visual impact if the use of texture is not controlled.

In the mural, "Mary, Mary, Quite Contrary, How Does Your Garden Grow", notice how the colours, sizes and shapes of the trees and flowers combine to form visual texture. They are "visually-busy" areas.

To contrast with these areas, it is essential, if a good design is to result, to leave some visually restful areas. These have been achieved in the path, sky, tree trunks and in the figure of Mary.

In a large activity, a good guide to effective visual results is this -

IF THE BACKGROUND IS VISUALLY TEXTURED, USE PLAIN FOREGROUND UNITS OR, IF THE FOREGROUND CONTAINS A LOT OF DETAIL, USE A PLAIN BACKGROUND.

One part of the display must dominate the other and the greater the domination, the stronger the visual effect.

When both foreground and background are equally textured or detailed, they compete with each other for the spectators' attention and, consequently, bring about a state of visual confusion in which the spectator experiences difficulty in identifying the detail.

* Make a collection of pictures or illustrations which show evidence of visual texture.

 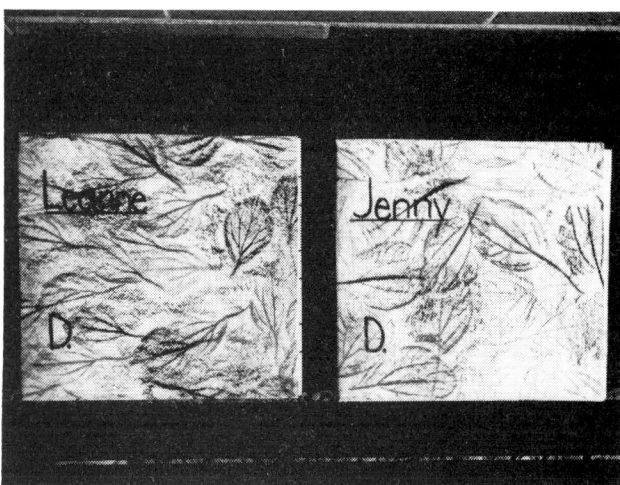

* Record a series of "rubbings" by placing a sheet of paper over a textured surface and rubbing a soft pencil or wax crayon over the paper. This process records a tactile texture as a visual texture.

* Experiment with ways of creating texture by drawing dots, lines or shapes.

* Make textures by pressing objects into soft clay or plasticine.

* Create textures by printing with foam plastic, crumpled newspaper, cardboard scraps, odds and ends; or by spatter painting, finger painting, splash painting.

* Many interesting textures can be created by applying other materials to the surface of a mural.

In the example above, the blossom trees have been represented by sprinkling confetti over the areas of wet adhesive.

The visual effect produced generally relates directly to the size of the material being applied, i.e., fine material produces a smooth texture, and course material, a rough texture.

Useful materials include -
Crushed egg shell   Fabric scraps
Styro-foam pieces   Crumpled paper
Wood shavings   Curled paper
Sawdust   Fringed paper
Cotton-wool   Wool

DEVELOPING PERCEPTUAL AWARENESS.....

So far in this book we have established the fact that all experience comes to us through our senses and particularly through our sense of vision. The various forms of visual experience such as colour, shape, line and texture have been explained.
Building on this foundation of visual experience, teachers can explore with the children the three basic avenues of developing perceptual awareness. That is, the three basic processes by which children can be made aware of the objects they encounter in their environment.

These are -

* AWARENESS THROUGH EXAMINING THE DETAIL OF AN OBJECT

* AWARENESS THROUGH AN EXPERIENCE INVOLVING THE USE OF THE OBJECT

* AWARENESS THROUGH IDENTIFICATION, IN THE SENSE THAT THE OBSERVER BECOMES THE OBJECT

These three principles can be applied to any tangible object and from their implementation will emerge many opportunities in which handwork activities can provide the kinds of experience and involvement which lead the child to a new and greater depth of understanding.
To illustrate the three points listed, assume that the object is a tree.

* AWARENESS THROUGH DETAIL — have the children investigate:

What shape the leaves are?
Do the leaves fall in winter?
Are the leaves large or small?
Do the leaves have a smell?
What colour the leaves are?
Is the bark smooth or rough?
Do birds nest in the tree?

How tall the tree is?
Can they stretch their arms around the tree?
Does the tree have a lot of branches?
Would it be easy to climb?
Can the sky be seen through the leaves?

* AWARENESS THROUGH EXPERIENCE — Have the children:

Visited a nursery?
Walked through a forest?
Planted a tree?
Chopped down a dead tree?
Picked a bunch of leaves?
Watched leaves change colour and fall off a tree?

Climbed a tree?
Built a tree house?
Visited a saw-mill?
Raked up leaves?
Pressed some leaves?
Discovered a bird's nest in a tree?

* AWARENESS THROUGH IDENTIFICATION — Can the children imagine:

Blowing in a strong wind?
Having birds nest in their branches?
Being burnt in a fire?
Watching their friends being cut down?
Losing their leaves?
Having caterpillars eat their leaves?

Being struck by lightning?
Being pushed over by a bulldozer?
Standing still on a cold, clear night?
Being so thirsty their leaves started to wilt?
Having children play in their branches?
Scattering their leaves to make a colourful carpet?

AWARENESS THROUGH DETAIL — FIND OUT:

Shape of the fish? Does it have teeth? Are the scales large? What colour is it? How many fins? Large or small mouth?	Colour of the feathers? Shape of the beak? Does it whistle? Large or small bird? Can it fly? What does it eat?	How many legs? Does it smell? Colour of the wings? Can it fly? Hard or soft wings? Shape of feelers?

AWARENESS THROUGH EXPERIENCE — HAVE YOU:

Caught a fish? Felt its slippery scales? Eaten a fish dinner? Watched fish in shallow water? Visited an aquarium? Fed fish?	Watched birds fly high in the sky? Kept a pet bird? Fed birds in a park? Held a bird in your hand? Cared for a sick bird? Watched birds build a nest?	Tried to catch a beetle? Held a beetle on your hand? Seen a collection of beetles? Listened to the song Alexander Beetle? Looked for beetles in the garden? Had a beetle race?

AWARENESS THROUGH IDENTIFICATION — IMAGINE

Being caught on a line. Swimming with other fish. Being eaten by bigger fish. People watching you in an aquarium. Being trapped in a net. Being out of the water.	Soaring high above the tree tops. Having to eat worms. Being kept in a cage. A cat is chasing you. Having to sit on eggs to hatch them. People throwing stones at you.	Sitting on a flower in the sun. Being trapped in a spider's web. Having poison sprayed on you. Crawling over a flower. Birds eating you. Being put in a glass jar and taken to school.

ACHIEVING INTEGRATION THROUGH HANDWORK.....

In formulating the basic philosophy of this book, it has been suggested that handwork activities provide a means of achieving three objectives -

Using the children's senses in the acquisition of cognitive development.
Establishing an awareness of visual forms through an appreciation of colour, shape, line and texture.
Developing an awareness of the things children encounter in their environment, this development being achieved by examining detail, experiencing situations, and identifying with the object or theme encountered.

To the progressive educator, the use of handwork activities solely as a means of achieving the development of a specific skill or technique, has become the exception rather than the rule.

Teachers are becoming increasingly aware of the numerous areas of the curriculum contributing to the development of concepts from and through handwork. Indeed, it will often occur that new techniques and skills will arise from the need to represent a particular texture, colour or form appropriate to the specific task at hand. However, this should be seen as a part of the total process of education, in which subject content, skills, techniques and materials find expression through the child's interpretation of the learning situation.

To examine in closer detail how this process might be put into practice, consider the theme of "The Sea" and the contribution several subject areas make to this topic.

Bearing in mind the fact that all experiences should be appropriate to the chronological and intellectual stage of development of the children concerned, it is most probable that a Natural Science experience will be used to introduce the theme. During the discussion, the various forms of life that exist in the sea might be identified, together with an understanding of the overall ecology of the sea.

A more detailed analysis of the theme would reveal the concept of the "food chain", identify forms of marine vegetation or lead to a classification of species of fish.

On the other hand, it might be just as appropriate to adopt a Social Science based inquiry into the ways man uses the sea for his own purpose. Areas of investigation might include:-

The challenge of the sea to early explorers and the types of ships used in voyages of discovery.

How man still uses the sea as a recovery or "soft landing area" for spacecraft returning from their voyages of discovery.

The sea as an area for recreational activity such as swimming, fishing, sailing, boating and diving.

The extensive tourist industry which makes the use of the sea-ways to the numerous holiday resorts of the Pacific Islands.

A classification of the variety of ships which use the seas e.g., Tugs, Fishing Trawlers, Cargo and Container Ships, Survey and Drilling Rigs, Naval Defence Ships, etc.

Dumping rubbish in the sea.

The sea as a source of food, and an examination of the methods by which it is harvested.

An examination of the dangers of the sea such as sharks, waves and tidal currents, storms at sea, poisonous forms of marine life.

Safety and the sea (frequently discussed in association with the previous topic) in which children might consider the provision of lighthouses to warn shipping of dangerous reefs or landforms, the general hazards of boating and fishing, especially the practice of fishing from rocks where unexpected waves could wash fishermen into the sea, etc.

Based on ideas which have emerged from discussion related to some of these topics, children have prepared the two examples shown.
In the first we see the children's representation of a group of swimmers enjoying a dip on a hot summer's day.

The second reveals several ideas. The lighthouse warning ships of dangerous rocks, fish swimming in schools and a fishing trawler using its big net to catch tuna fish.
Many other subject areas can extend the children's experiences in other areas of the general theme. For example, the children might participate in a cooking activity which makes use of seafoods. Dishes such as tuna patties, fish fingers, sweet and sour tuna or tuna mornay can be prepared with a minimum of equipment.
An art experience can give form to the aesthetic qualities of the sea and associated objects, such as shells, sponges, seaweed and rock, emphasising the colours, shapes, textures and linear qualities that the children observe in these things.
As well as reading stories and poems which relate to the sea, other English experiences such as creative writing, drama and the overall development of the children's capacity for oral communication through their contribution to discussion on aspects of the topic, will provide effective integration.
The sea is just one example of how many subject areas contribute to the children's understanding of a particular theme.
In the pages that follow many ideas and approaches have been suggested. However, it must be stressed again that these activities are not intended to be used exclusively for the development of Handwork skills, but rather that through the children's involvement in ideas, information and activities related to the various topics, there will emerge greater understanding, increased interest and the desire to learn more about the world in which they live.
In all activities, the essential thing to remember is that the "end product" is of little importance: it is the experience gained from participating in activities which contribute significantly to the child's total education that determines the relevance of Handwork.

WELCOME TO OUR CLASSROOM . . . . .

The classroom door is the first real encounter that children, parents and visitors have with the classroom, so why not make it a bright, friendly, display area? Here are some ideas.

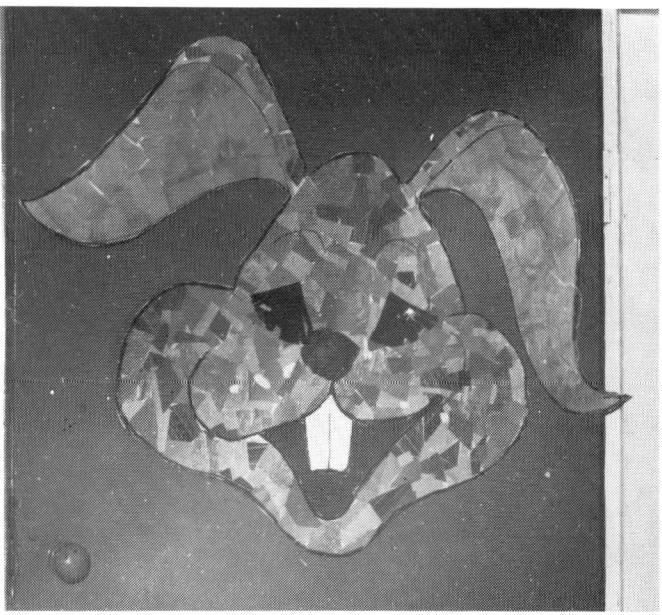

ENVIRONMENTAL INFLUENCE.....

In these two activites, notice how the children's environment has influenced their work.
Three dimensional units have been used to represent the buildings surrounding Sydney Harbour while, in the second activity, children have captured the speed and excitement of a sailing race on Lake Macquarie.

It's windy out on the lake today,

BLACK AND WHITE.....

Frequently, unusual and dramatic visual effects can be achieved by the emphasis of contrast. The juxtapostion of black and white provides the maximum contrast so it is a natural conclusion that penguins and zebras are two obvious subjects to use for this theme. On this page examples of two and three dimensional approaches to the topic, "Penguins of Macquarie Island", have been shown. Useful materials to suggest the ice flow include cotton wool and small pieces of styrofoam. Penguins, if painted black on the back, make an effective mobile.

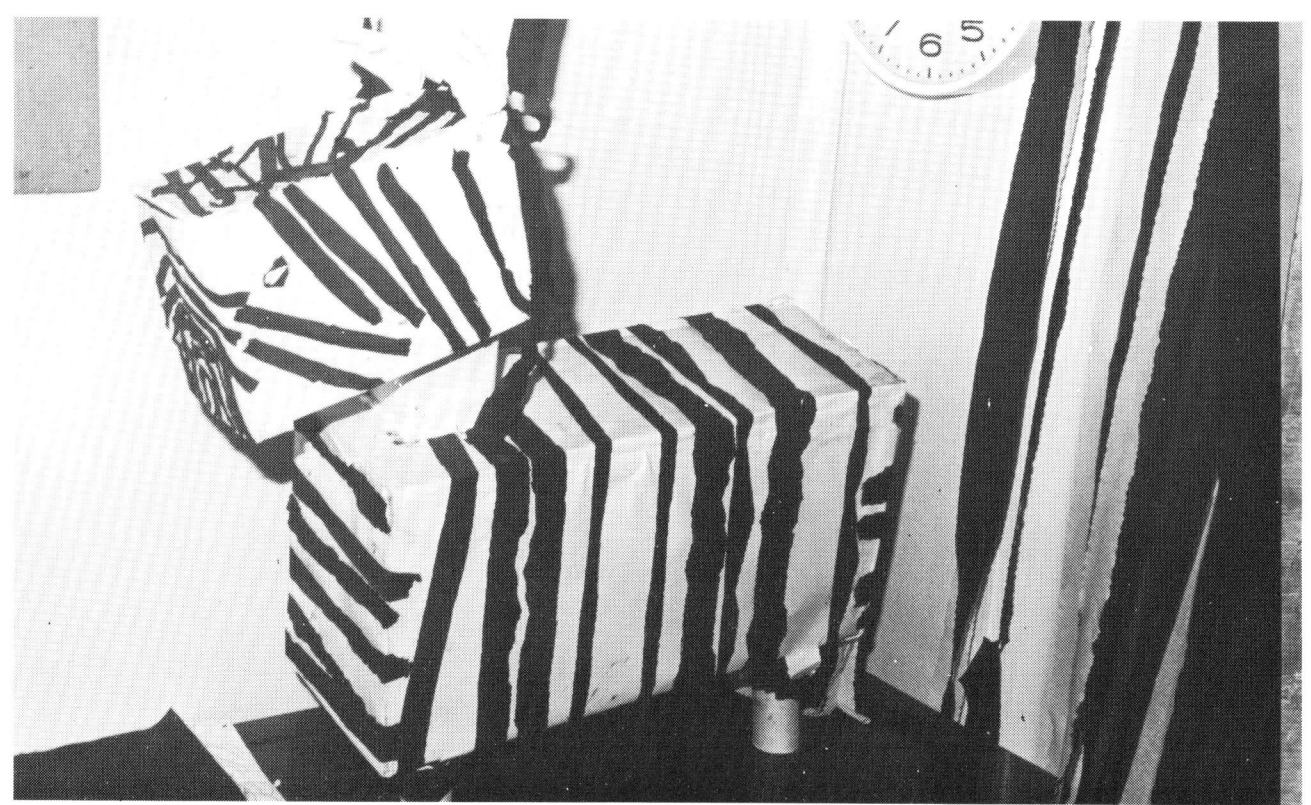

Many activities such as the penguin in the mobile and the zebra below can be made as a "pillow" model.

This is achieved by cutting two identical shapes. One forms the front and the other the back. The shapes are glued or stapled around the edges, leaving a small opening at one point through which padding in the form of crumpled newspaper is inserted. When the required thickness has been established the opening is sealed. The result — a three dimensional form from a two dimensional beginning.

SPEAKING OF COWS . . . . .

✱ The head of the friendly cow on the previous page can be used as an introduction to a host of activities. Apart from being used to illustrate the following poem, it can form the starting point for themes related to the Dairy Industry, Where Our Food Comes From, Foods to Keep Us Healthy, etc.

SPEAKING OF COWS

Speaking of cows
Which we really weren't doing,
Why do they stand there
Staring and chewing?

Once in a while
You hear a cow mooing,
Swishing her tail
At a fly that needs shooing.

Staring at people
Chewing at clover,
Doing the same things
Over and over.

Most of the time though
What are cows doing,
Munching and looking
Staring and chewing.

Cows just don't care for
New ways of doing
That's what they stare for
That's why they're chewing

✱ Use the fold-cut technique set out below to make some cows to illustrate "Speaking of Cows".

1. Fold the paper in half. Note: Variations in size will produce a better class display.

2. Sketch in "bell" shape of head then add ears and horns. Cut waste away.

3. Unfold cut shape of head. Draw in expression. Cut slit for mouth if required.

✱ Attach cow-heads to bodies with paper fasteners. This will allow the heads to be moved into various positions.

✱ Prepare a poster showing how milk is processed and distributed.

✱ An alternate method of making cows is by folding them as shown below.

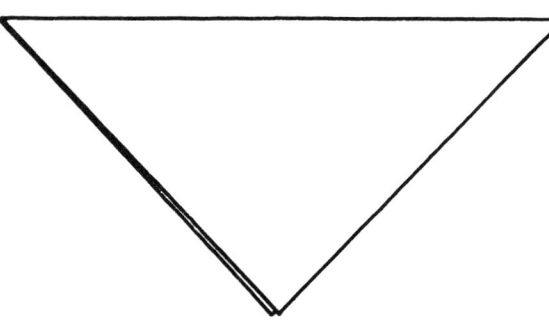

1. Start with a square of paper and fold it diagonally in half.

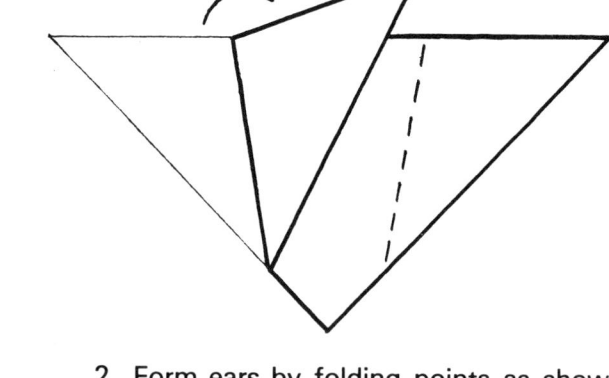

2. Form ears by folding points as shown. The second point will overlap the first.

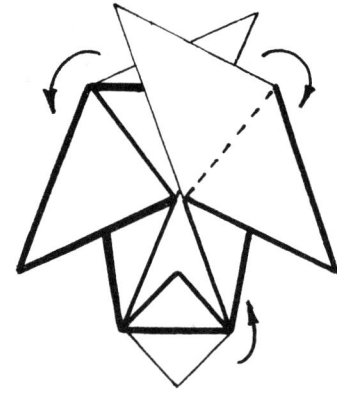

3. Complete ears by folding ends back in the opposite direction. Fold chin under. Continue folding as indicated by the arrows. Illustration shows the back surface of the head.

4. Glue on horns and nose. These are cut from separate pieces of paper.

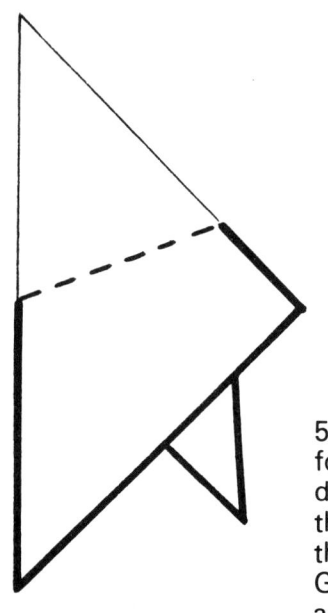

5. To make the body, fold a square of paper diagonally in half and then fold again so that the points form the feet. Glue head to body. Add a tail for effect.

* Food and where it comes from can lead to a wide variety of activities. Apart from examining the original source of the food and how it is processed, the children should be given the opportunity to experience some of the food by participating in cooking activities. Here are additional ideas -

Wheat farming - Cook some bread
Chicken farming - Cook some eggs
Fishing Industry - Prepare a seafood dish
Fruit Industry - Make some toffee apples.

HEALTH AND SAFETY . . . . .

* A natural extension of an investigation of the various types of food is the classification of those which promote good health.

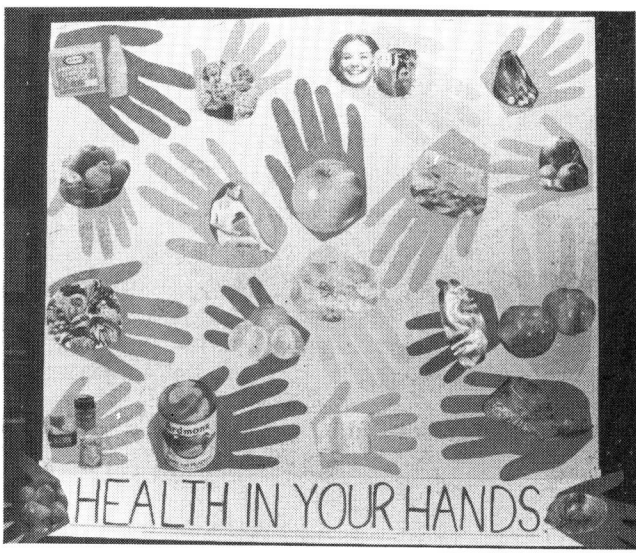

MAGIC . . . . .

Children always respond with interest and enthusiasm to the performance of magic tricks, so try these simple ideas with your class.

* MAGIC BRUSH AND INK

Tell the children your "magic" brush and ink will show them the spelling words for the week. (Actually any type of material can be introduced in this way).

Before the lesson, print the words on a sheet of stiff white paper with a white wax crayon. The words will not be readily visible until the paper is brushed with "magic" ink. The wax will repel the ink and the words will appear. The "magic" ink is any dark coloured ink or very thin paint.

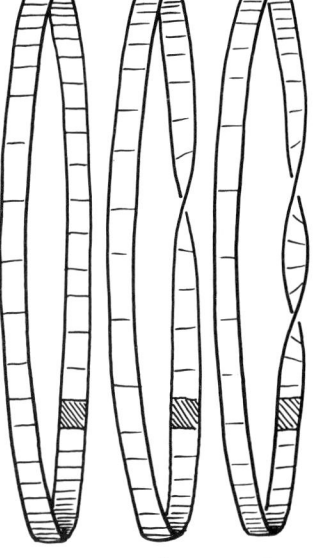

* MAGIC PAPER HOOPS

From three different coloured strips of crepe paper about 8 cm. wide and 2 metres long, prepare three hoops. The first should be a simple circle. In the second, form a half twist before glueing the ends together and, in the third, a full twist. Place all three hoops in a paper bag prior to presenting the trick.

Select three children and give them a pair of "magic" scissors. Ask one child to select a hoop (the colour which you have prepared as No. 1) and cut along the middle of it. As expected this will make two hoops.

1. 2. 3.

Now ask two other children to cut along the middle of the other two hoops. To their surprise they will find one is a very large hoop and the other is one hoop threaded through another.

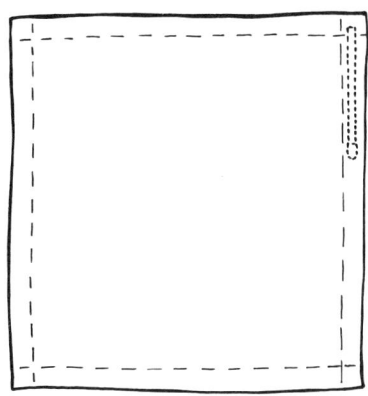

* BROKEN MATCH TRICK

Hide a match in the hem of a large handkerchief.

Now, to present the trick, select a child and ask him to place a match in the centre of the handkerchief. Gather the hemline around the match so as to cover the match and, at the same time, bring the hidden match into a position that it can be felt through the centre of the handkerchief. Ask another child to help break the match he can feel. (Actually he is breaking the hidden match).

Next tell the children that you will mend the broken match by waving a bottle of glue over the handkerchief. Give the handkerchief a shake and the unbroken match will fall onto the table. The broken pieces of the other match remain hidden in the hem.

WITCHES .....

* Introduce this theme by telling the children that people in olden times thought witches were strange creatures with powers of magic that were capable of casting strange spells.

In the illustration below, the striking silhouette effect has been achieved by cutting the shapes from a sheet of thick opaque paper and superimposing this on tissue or cellophane. The finished unit is displayed agaist a window pane.

THE WITCH

I saw her picking daisies,
And marked her where she stood,
She didn't know I watched her
While hiding in the wood.

Her skirt was brilliant crimson
And black her pointed hat,
Her broomstick lay beside her,
I'm very sure of that.

Her chin was sharp and pointed,
Her eyes were - I don't know -
For when she turned towards me,
I thought it best to go.

A FUNNY OLD WITCH

Swishing its tail, the witch's cat,
Lean and sleek, by the cauldron sat,
The pine burned bright and the wind blew cold,
And spells were strong in the days of old.
Now by the fire the black cats lie
And swish their tails when the wind blows high
Their green eyes dream of the dark nights ride,
When they flew to the stars by the witch's side.

THE WITCH'S CAT

A funny old witch in a black pointed cap,
Knocked on my door with a rap, rap, rap,
When I opened the door to see who was there,
She jumped on her broomstick and flew
                    through the air.

N.B. In this unit the textured effect has been produced by finger painting the window pane.
The linear shapes have been spot glued over the background.

THE OLD WOOD WITCH

The old wood witch, she rides by night,
Across the sky, an eerie sight,
She sits on her broom with her pointed hat,
Her black flowing robes and of course, her cat.
Her nose is hooked and her face looks old,
Her chin is sharp, with a wart, I'm told,
Her fingers are thin and bony and strong
Her nails are very, very long.
So beware, beware for the moon is new,
Stay out of her path or she may curse you.

THE WITCH'S HOUSE

A funny old house at the edge of the wood,
Is the home of an ugly old witch,
Who all the day long mixes magic spells,
In a cauldron as black as pitch.

A few handy witch-forms

MAKE SOME MICE.....

*Single or double units of egg cartons provide a useful means of modelling mice (see next page), however, when these are used, it is difficult to introduce any variation into the size of the mice. A very effective alternate method is to fold them from paper.

These paper mice can be integrated with many activities such as mice as pets, stories, poems and songs about mice or, made from large size paper, they can be used as party or fancy-dress hats.

1. Fold a rectangle 9 cm by 12 cm (or similar proportion) in half.

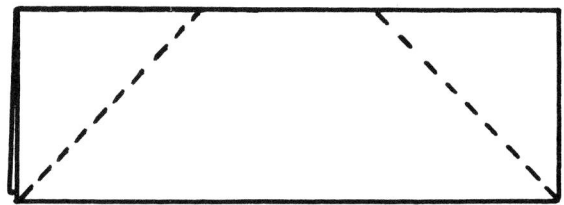

2. With fold uppermost, fold each end over at 45° to crease paper and open back out again.

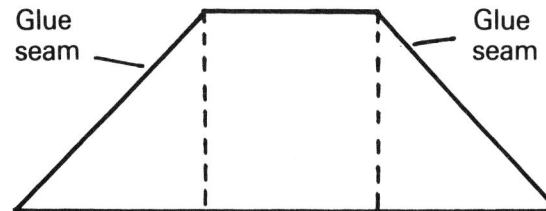

3. Tuck the area above the crease back inside the main area by reversing the fold. Do this at each end. Glue seam together.

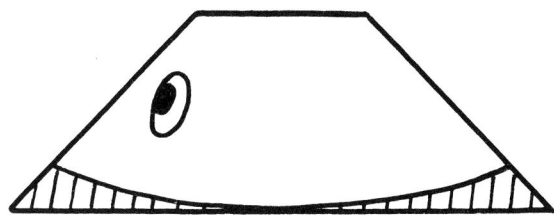

4. Cut curved line to remove waste area. Twist a single crepe paper bow for ears and a short length of crepe paper for the tail.

61

An extremely useful technique, which can be applied in a number of ways, is that used in the above activity to produce a three-dimensional effect from a flat surface.

The faces of the mice have been made by cutting a circle from thin cardboard with two smaller circles being used to represent the ears. The three-dimensional effect is achieved by cutting along a radius of the circle and then overlapping the surfaces to form a low-profile cone.

The furry surface is produced by covering the cone with layers of fringed paper. Start from the outside edge and work towards the centre, finishing in the centre with a circle of fringed crepe paper.

This same 3D technique has been used on the face of the rabbit shown opposite, the only difference being that the original shape is no longer a circle but rather the actual face. The 3D effect is achieved by cutting down the centre of the head to the nose and overlapping as before.

Here are some additional ideas for integrating with the mice shown on the previous page.

A MOUSE'S LETTER TO SANTA

A wee mouse wrote to Santa Claus
   And this is what he said,
"I write this letter Santa Claus,
   To ask for cheese and bread,
But if it just should happen,
   That you're short of either, please,
Just give the bread to someone else,
   And send along the cheese".

* Illustrate the story of the Pied Piper.

POEMS AND RHYMES.....

* Most poems and rhymes lend themselves to presentation as a theme for handwork activities. Here are some examples.

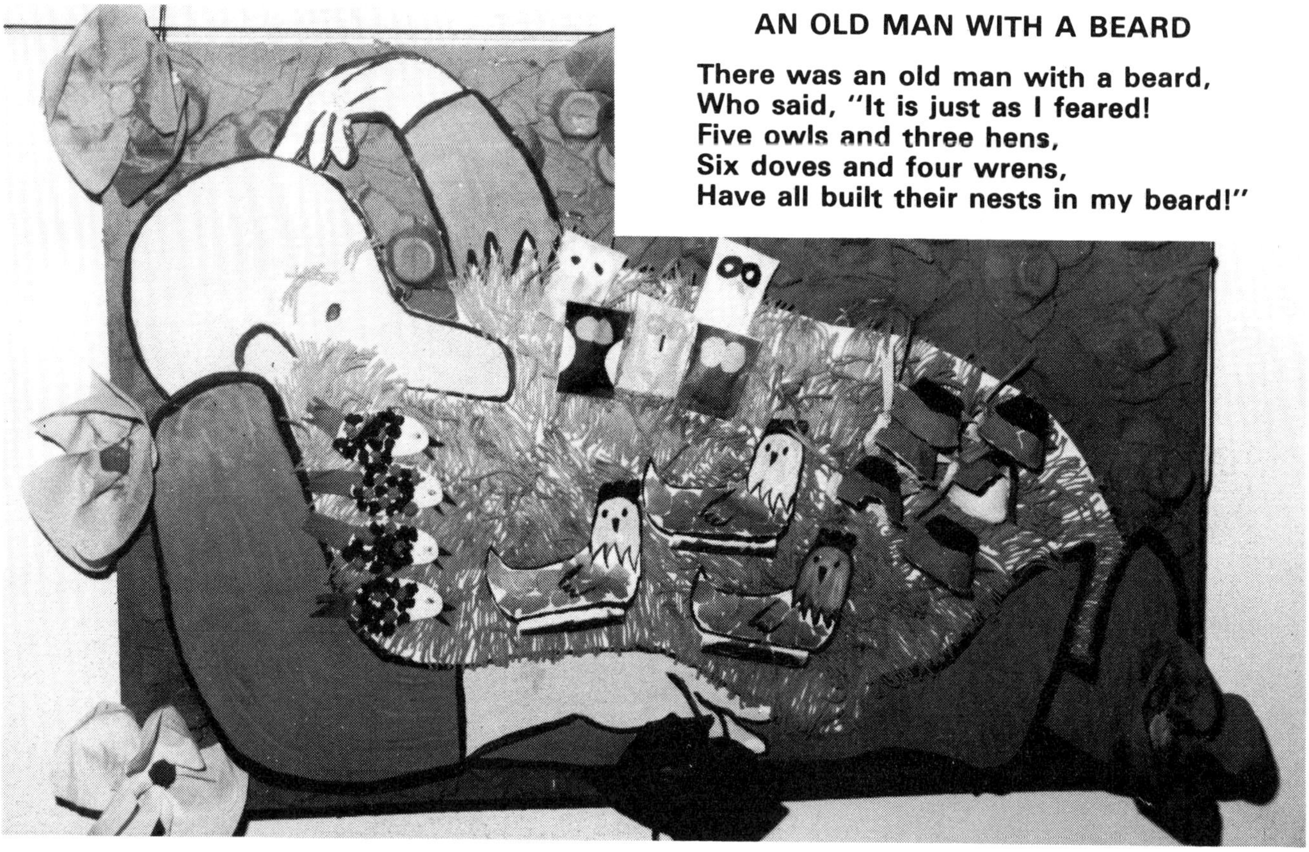

AN OLD MAN WITH A BEARD

There was an old man with a beard,
Who said, "It is just as I feared!
Five owls and three hens,
Six doves and four wrens,
Have all built their nests in my beard!"

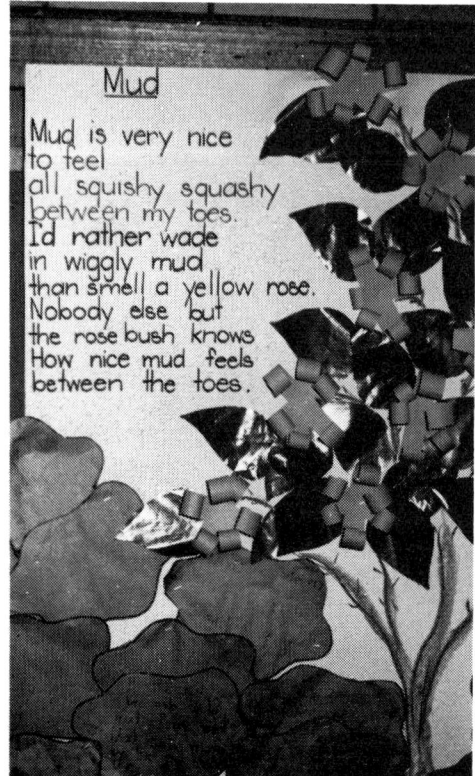

MR. PELICAN

Surely, Mr. Pelican,
Your bill is a mistake,
"I find it very useful
For fishing in the lake".

RABBITS

Rabbits here and rabbits there,
   See the rabbits everywhere,
Hopping gaily in the grass,
   In among the trees they pass.
Tramp, tramp, hark, hark,
   Man's step, dog's bark,
Comes the hunter with his gun,
Rabbits vanish everyone.

LIGHTHOUSE

I'd like to be a lighthouse
   All scrubbed and painted white,
I'd like to be a lighthouse,
   And shine my light at night,
I'd keep a watch on everything
   That sails on past my door,
And warn of hidden danger
   Along the rocky shore.

MR. GIRAFFE

Mr. Giraffe you are such a laugh,
   You seem to look all wrong,
Your head is so high up there in the sky,
   And your neck is so very long,
It seems to me, that your dinner and tea
   Have such a long way to go
I'm wondering how, they manage to know,
   The way to your tummy below.

FROGS CHORUS

We had a sudden storm today,
  With wind and heavy rain,
And now the creeks and waterholes
  Are all filled up again.

So through my open window,
  I hear the frogs rejoice,
And every different kind of frog
  Has quite a different voice.

Attach feet to body shape with units of pleated paper.

PETS AND ANIMALS.....

MY DOG SPOT

I have a little dog
  Whose name is Spot,
Sometimes he's white
  And sometimes he's not.

But whether he's white
  Or whether he's not,
The patches all over him
  Tell me he's Spot.

He likes a bone,
  And he likes a ball,
But he doesn't care
  For cats at all.

He lies in the sun,
  And waits all day,
For school to finish
  So we can play.

✻ Use the poem to introduce the theme of pets. Discuss the types of pets children keep at home. Prepare a graph of the results as shown on the next page.
Using paper fasteners to assemble the parts, have the children make animated dogs like Spot.

2ND CLASS GRAPH OF THEIR PETS.....

dogs	cats	fish	birds	others

* Children draw their pet on a separate sheet of paper, cut around the shape and glue it to the appropriate bar of the graph.

Another approach to developing themes which relate to animals is to examine the types of animals found on a farm. Depending on the purpose and depth of the inquiry, children may discuss the nature of the commodity supplied by the different animals, such as meat, wool, milk, eggs, bacon, etc., or they may investigate the role of animals on the farm, e.g., dogs to round up sheep, horses as a form of transport, stud animals for breeding.

* Frequently however, involvement may be in relation to a story or song about a farm. This is the case in the illustration of Old MacDonald's Farm, shown below.

As a point of interest, notice how three skirt hangers have been used to support the mural, a useful technique when brick or glass surfaces limit appropriate display surfaces.

※ Extending the theme of farm animals, the activities on this page suggest approaches which combine fun rhymes with some of the farm animals.

THE COW
The friendly cow, all black and white,
   I love with all my heart,
She gives me cream with all her might,
   To eat with apple tart.

THE PIG
The pig, if I am not mistaken,
   Supplies us sausages, ham and bacon,
Let others say his heart is big,
   I call it foolish of the pig.

THE PURPLE COW
I've never seen a purple cow,
   I hope I never see one.
But I can tell you anyhow,
   I'd rather see than be one.

MOTHER HEN
"Now see here," said the mother hen
   From her farm-yard patch,
If you want your breakfast,
   Just come out here and scratch.

* Notice the relationship of the diet of the Three Pigs, above, to the construction of their homes. This is one appoach to relating animals to a unit on health education.

* Many ideas will emerge from an excursion to a place of special interest and this activity is one such example. It represents a follow-up unit constructed after the children have visited a Lion Park.

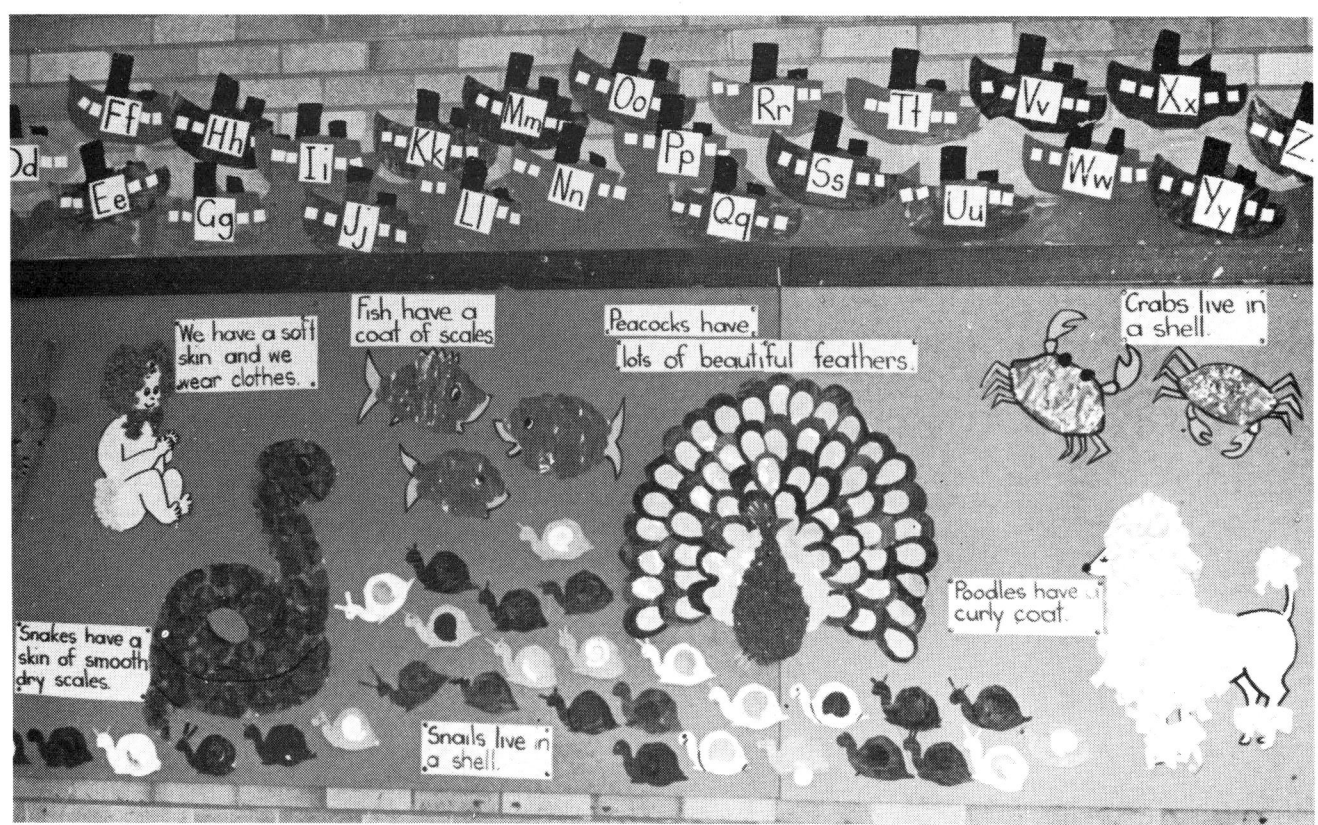

  ✱ Observations of animals can be represented in many ways and, in the examples on this page, emphasis has been placed on an examination of their types of covering. This approach provides opportunities for children to discuss the colours and textures of the coverings as well as identifying their function, such as providing warmth (feathers and fur), provide protection (scales and shell) or, as in the case of the peacock, to attract attention.

EASTER ACTIVITIES . . . . .

* Many seasonal or specific themes occur during the year, of which Easter is just one example. Most activities which relate to an Easter theme tend to be three dimensional with the result that many really effective units can be constructed from cones and cylinders. Several examples are shown below.

An extremely useful material for many of these units is aluminium foil. Forms for eggs can be made by crumpling newspaper to the required size and shape and covering this core with the aluminum foil.

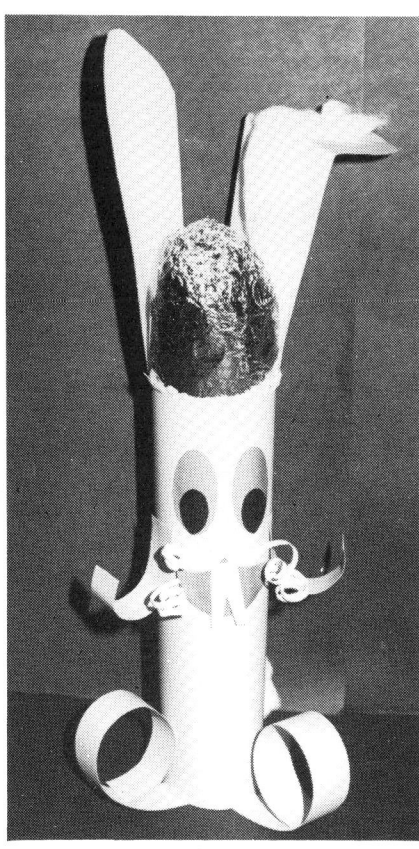

* In the units below, the hen has been made by glueing two shapes together around the edges and padding with crumpled newspaper. An empty egg carton with the top area removed forms the body of the rabbit. This has been covered with strips of fringing, and the feet, face and a fluffy tail are added to complete the unit.

USING SCRAP MATERIALS . . . . .

As the cost of handwork materials increases steadily, teachers are turning to a wide variety of scrap materials to supplement their supply of traditional items.

Scrap materials have many distinct advantages to offer, for, apart from the individual variations of colours, shapes, sizes and textures, the actual nature of the materials themselves will often provide valuable opportunities for problem solving experiences. Children must constantly assess the strength of the materials to see if it is suitable to meet the needs of the project on which they are engaged. They must consider the types of construction or identify the form of adhesive most appropriate to the task at hand.

In many major cities, teachers are encouraging the use of scrap materials through participation in a scheme referred to as "The Reverse Garbage Truck". In essence, this scheme provides for the bulk collection from manufacturing industries of waste materials such as offcuts, stampings, oddments and other units unsuitable for commercial use. These materials are sorted and stored in a central distribution area where, for a nominal subscription proportional to the number of children attending the school, teachers can select a range of materials for use in their handwork activities.

There are several approaches to the use of scrap materials -

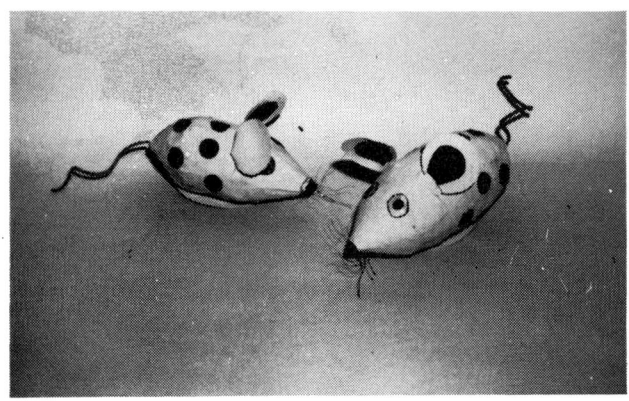

1. The first is an individual approach where children are given the opportunity to work with a specific type of scrap. For example, each child may be provided with an empty egg carton and encouraged to work towards the construction of a pre-determined idea such as a caterpillar, bee, butterfly, spider, mouse, owl, etc.
Similar activities may centre on the use of other specific items such as cardboard cylinders, paper plates, paper bags or fabric scraps.

2. In the second approach, emphasis is placed on a specific theme or subject. Here a wider range of scrap materials is used to contribute to the expression of the theme. Television Station, Robot, Puppets for a Puppet Play, Types of Transport, Kinder's Cake Shop, Spaceship, A Giant Dragon, Adventure Playhouse, are just a few examples of the thematic approach.

3. The third approach is simply to expose children to a range of materials in order that they may use their own innate creativity to give form to ideas from their own experience. When very young children are engaged in the latter approach it is important to remember that the finished product may not necessarily assume any recognisable form. Don't ask "What is it?" It may just be that it isn't anything at all, other than an experience in glueing, joining or supporting, or simply an indulgence in the sheer joy of making.

In planning the use of scrap materials, the most important thing to remember is that children need to be exposed to a range of experiences rather than an overindulgence in just one. By adopting this procedure, all areas of the child's development will be enhanced. Skills will be developed through working towards specific goals; social development will occur through involvement in a co-operative venture with others; and the development of individual creativity will be fostered through the opportunity to use materials in an innovative and expressive manner.

To represent the characters in the story, "Snow White and the Seven Dwarfs", children used a variety of scrap materials to make their puppets. In the background is a scene representing the wood; another scene representing the wicked Queen's castle is also part of the activity.

As well as gaining experience in the skills required to make their puppets the children gain valuable experience from the actual presentation of "Snow White" as a puppet play.

DISPLAY TECHNIQUE

Shown opposite is an extremely useful idea for displaying units related to a Circus theme.
Strips of cardboard have been glued to form a circus ladder, from which the clowns faces have been displayed. As both sides of the ladder can be used, this technique provides an effective three dimensional form of display.

MAKE A CAKE SHOP.....

* As well as providing an opportunity for children to use a variety of scrap materials in a novel and imaginative way, this activity also leads to the development of number concepts through the children's participation in shopping play or the use of number work cards which set out simple problems based on the items available in the "cake shop".

ICED CAKES
Paint single egg carton units to represent icing. Top with a crumpled paper "cherry".

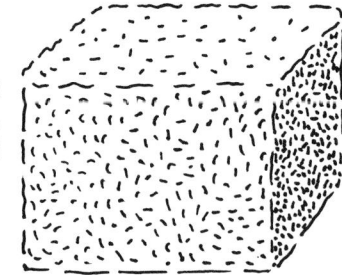

COCONUT CAKES
Cut cubes of foam plastic, paint chocolate colour and sprinkle with sawdust.

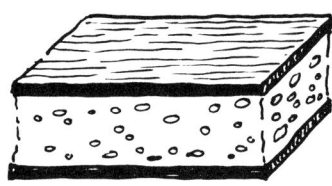

VANILLA SLICE
Glue cardboard "pastry" to foam-plastic filling.

CHOCOLATE CRACKLES
Crumple crepe paper and glue into a patty cake paper.

ROCK CAKES
Make papier mache shapes. Press crumpled paper currants into the surface.

CREAM TARTS
Fill units from tray-pak apple spacers with cotton wool or crumpled paper "cream".

JAM ROLLS
Prepare rolls from pieces of corrugated cardboard with filling of thin foam plastic or cotton wool. Paint the cardboard an appropriate colour.

CAKES MADE TO ORDER
A special service of the Cake Shop can be cakes made to order. Use half or full size egg cartons as the base of the cake. Decorate with paints and trim with a fringed edging.

* A convenient means of displaying the various cakes is to use several plastic throw-away trays (used for packing meat and fruit in supermarkets) or the lids of ice-cream cans in which a paper doiley has been glued. Make price tags to indicate cost of cakes.

HANDWORK IS SOMETHING TO SING ABOUT.....

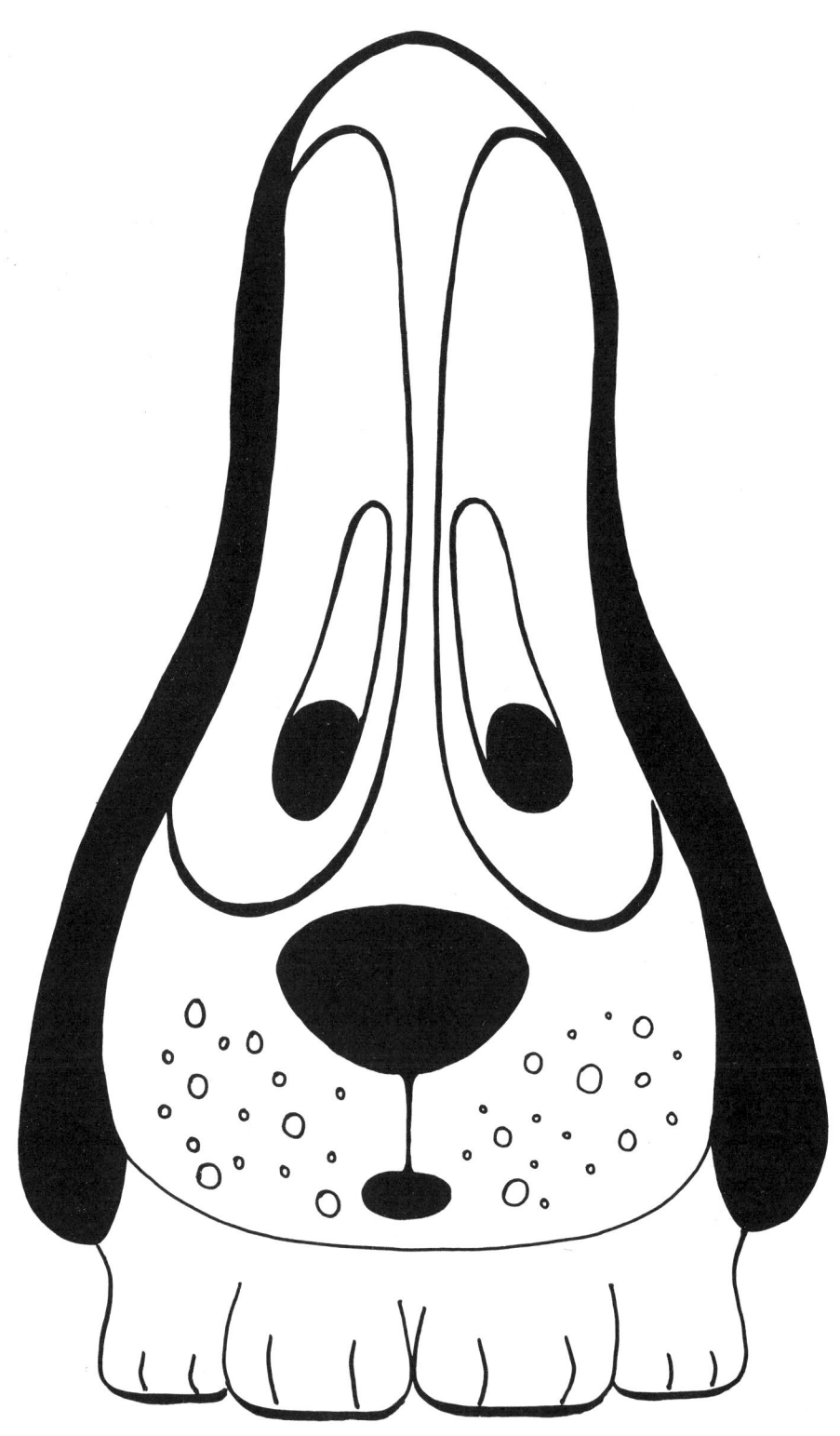

FOR DETAILS OF OTHER BELAIR PUBLICATIONS WRITE TO:
BELAIR PUBLICATIONS LIMITED
PO BOX 12
TWICKENHAM TW1 2QL
ENGLAND